TAKING COLLEGE TEACHING SERIOUSLY: PEDAGOGY MATTERS!

Taking College Teaching Seriously:
Pedagogy Matters!

Fostering Student Success Through Faculty-Centered Practice Improvement

Gail O. Mellow, Diana D. Woolis,
Marisa Klages-Bombich, and
Susan G. Restler

Foreword by Rosemary Arca

STERLING, VIRGINIA

Published by Stylus Publishing, LLC
22883 Quicksilver Drive
Sterling, Virginia 20166-2102

Library of Congress Cataloging-in-Publication Data

Mellow, Gail O'Connor.
Taking college teaching seriously : pedagogy matters! / by Gail
O. Mellow, Diana D. Woolis, Marisa Klages-Bombich and Susan
Restler.
  pages cm
Includes bibliographical references and index.
ISBN 978-1-62036-079-8 (cloth : alk. paper)
ISBN 978-1-62036-080-4 (pbk. : alk. paper)
ISBN 978-1-62036-081-1 (library networkable e-edition)
ISBN 978-1-62036-082-8 (consumer e-edition)
1. College teaching. 2. Critical pedagogy. I. Title.
LB2331.M4425 2015
378.1'25–dc23
                                                    2014048776

13-digit ISBN: 978-1-62036-079-8 (cloth)
13-digit ISBN: 978-1-62036-080-4 (paperback)
13-digit ISBN: 978-1-62036-081-1 (library networkable e-edition)
13-digit ISBN: 978-1-62036-082-8 (consumer e-edition)

Printed in the United States of America

All first editions printed on acid-free paper
that meets the American National Standards Institute
Z39-48 Standard.

Bulk Purchases

Quantity discounts are available for use in workshops and for
staff development.
Call 1-800-232-0223

First Edition, 2015

10   9   8   7   6   5   4   3   2   1

Dedicated to the thousands of teaching faculty who create magic every day in classes across the country for the students who need them.

CONTENTS

ACKNOWLEDGMENTS

This project comes from the collective energy, wisdom, and research of the faculty who created the pedagogy matters practice improvement model in Cohort 1: Peter Adams, Community College of Baltimore County, MD; Rosemary Arca, Foothill College, CA; J. Elizabeth Clark, LaGuardia Community College, NY; Teresa DeMonico, Sinclair Community College, OH; Michael Dubson, Bunker Hill Community College, MA; Kristin Duckworth, Community College of Baltimore County, MD; Jason Evans, Prairie State College, IL; Richard Getso, South Texas College, TX; Yasser Hassebo, LaGuardia Community College, NY; Lori Hirst, St. Louis Community College at Forest Park, MO; Nancy Hoagland, Northern Virginia Community College–Alexandria Campus, VA; Eric Kraus, Sinclair Community College, OH; Bronte Miller, Patrick Henry Community College, VA; Katrina Nichols, Delta College, MI; Elizabeth Nicoli-Suco, Miami Dade College, FL; Trisha O'Connor, Delta College, MI; Robin Ozz, Phoenix College, AZ; Kathryn Perino, Foothill College, CA; Richard Pescarino, St. Louis Community College at Florissant Valley, MO; LaVache Scanlan, Kapi'olani Community College, HI; Terry Shamblin, Monroe Community College, NY; Kate Smith, Monroe Community College, NY; Reid Sunahara, Kapi'olani Community College, HI; Christopher Watson, Bunker Hill Community College, MA; Michelle Zollars, Patrick Henry Community College, VA. We cannot thank them enough.

Cohort 2 brought perspicacity and energy and tested the fledgling pedagogy matters process and helped to refine it: Steve Blount, Lewis and Clark Community College, CO; Valerie Cox, Calhoun Community College, AL; Chris DeDual, Mississippi Gulf Coast Community College; Claudia Delgado, Hudson County Community College, NJ; Misty Evans, Murray State University, KY; Stephanie Fernandes, Lewis and Clark Community College, IL; Larry Giddings, Pikes Peak Community College, CO; Kristen Good, Washtenaw Community College, MI; Arlene Heaster, Northeast Wisconsin Technical College, WI; Joyce Lindstrom, St. Charles Community College, MO; Douglas Mace, Kirtland Community College, MI; Teri Maddox, Jackson State Community College, TN; Laurie McCartan, Metropolitan State University, MN; Catherine Montero, Northern Virginia Community College–Loudoun Campus, VA; Judi Nistch, Harper College, IL; Mary Ann

Saurino, Inver Hills Community College, MN; Steve Schoenbaechler, Sinclair Community College, OH; Mike Sfiropoulos, Palm Beach State College, FL; Joan Smith, Calhoun Community College, AL; Monica Stansberry, El Centro Community College, TX; Brenda Tuberville, Rogers State University, OK; Dawn White, Davidson County Community College, NC; and Trisha White, Ozarks Technical College, MO. We are deeply grateful for their participation.

We also wish to acknowledge and thank all the individuals who believed in this project and worked to launch it. We want to especially thank Diane Troyer, of the Bill & Melinda Gates Foundation, who was the first to believe that taking college teaching seriously was an important part of the completion agenda, and Hillary Pennington, who agreed to move the project forward. We then had a series of great program officers at the Gates Foundation: Suzanne Walsh, Brock Grubb, and Bree Obrecht. The incomparable home team for Knowledge in the Public Interest included Lisa Levinson as the community manager par excellence; Laren Droll as the tech guru and whisperer; Stephanie Margolin as the extraordinary librarian; Brenda Kaulbach as the community facilitator; and Susan James as the in-house filmmaker. LaGuardia Community College's leaders included Paul Arcario, provost; Bret Eynon, dean; and a host of administrative support staff from LaGuardia's information technology, finance, and advancement offices.

We worked closely with Gerardo de los Santos and Stella Perez of the League for Innovation in the Community College during our first years. Our evaluators were Terri Manning and Dawn Coleman at the Center for Applied Research at Central Piedmont Community College; Louise Yarnall and her extensive team at SRI International, Mingyu Feng, Carolyn Dornsife, Anna Werner, Judith Fusco, Ellen Tidwell-Morgan, Federick Ngo, and Lawrence Gallagher; and Melanie Hwalek and her team from SPEC Associates, Natalie DeSole, Sally Bond, and Victoria Straub. Diana Laurillard, professor of learning with digital technologies at the London Knowledge Lab at the University of London was an early conceptual adviser. A tip of the hat to Andrea Kahn who came up with the title *Taking College Teaching Seriously: Pedagogy Matters! Fostering Student Success Through Faculty-Centered Practice Improvement*.

We are also grateful to Chera Reid and William Moses of The Kresge Foundation, who have funded a large-scale demonstration project as this book goes to print to establish a faculty focus as a part of their overall investment in college improvement.

Finally, although she is one of the authors, the amazing grace, multitasking, and the never-losing-a-single-detail capability of Marisa Klages-Bombich as the project director must be once again celebrated.

FOREWORD

In my penultimate year of teaching, I was asked to become part of a community of reflective practitioners focused on improving student success in developmental courses. I said *yes* emphatically.

The Global Skills for College Completion (GSCC) project, funded by the Bill & Melinda Gates Foundation, was framed by the belief that teaching mattered, that pedagogy was a determining factor in student success and college completion, and that a powerful set of tools and routines could enable teachers to shape lessons that would engage students and enable their learning. This happened via a process that included weekly reflection, peer feedback, and enlightened coaching by experienced teachers using Web 2.0 tools.

When I joined the project, I wanted the energy of collaboration, the challenges of feedback, and, finally, the creativity that comes from conversations with passionate teachers who love what they do. I wanted to get out of the office and talk to really smart people who delighted in imagining the best way to teach paragraph development or factoring polynomials. I wanted to be forced to reevaluate the routines I'd developed over 37 years of teaching, and I wanted to be challenged to try new technologies that might have some value to add in today's classroom.

For me, the process was heady and humbling. The weekly online posts about what we did in *one lesson in one class* and the reflection about that class were powerful meditations on what I was doing in the classroom. I had to be an honest reporter of my own practice by using the categories of reflection required by the project. I gained a deeper understanding of pedagogy and what worked (or didn't) in the lesson I'd taught and recorded. It was as if the act of documenting the work or naming the parts of the lesson actually highlighted areas where the lesson had been too teacher-centered or too general, where transitions interrupted student learning, or, the key to my own growth, where students had been confused. This was heady knowledge indeed.

The very humbling part of the process came when I entered my colleagues' virtual classrooms in my discipline and watched them teaching via video excerpts or their online postings. Then I noted the amazing proactivity of their lessons that demonstrated their knowledge of individual student issues and careful planning to enable student success. We GSCCers mined each other's posts for creative discussion strategies and effective classroom assessment techniques. Many of us completely restructured our lesson plans after we saw how powerful our colleagues' lessons were in ensuring that students mastered a concept in our discipline. I borrowed the appointment clock (a one-time scheduling of discussion pairs that we could use throughout the semester), the ticket out (a way to assess students' understanding before they leave the room), and the quote sandwich (a template easing students into the effective use of and commentary on quotations in an essay).

In our weekly circles, we posted our own reflections about a lesson, we read our circlemates' postings, and we helped our colleagues discern areas of strength and areas for growth. We used appreciative inquiry to set the focus and tone of our commentary by asking "what if" rather than saying "you should." These weekly cycles of observation and conversation helped identify patterns emerging in our teaching practice, and our GSCC community engaged us in considering what other patterns we might try. This recursive process reminded me that even our teaching brains needed to build new synapses, new ways to work, to maintain the effectiveness of our teaching.

Certainly, the identification of my teaching pattern was the most exciting experience of the practice. The pattern was derived from a process of highlighting and tagging my posted lessons and from the observations of my peers. In the first half of the semester we had collaboratively developed themes and tags in pedagogy. In the latter half of the project, we tagged our own posts and our circlemates' posts. For example, if we noticed an activity that seemed to create a supportive learning environment for students we tagged it *Comfort*. When we noted an activity that scaffolded study habits expected in college we tagged that *College Transition*. If we saw a lesson that required analysis, evaluation, or synthesis of text, we tagged it *Higher Order Thinking Skills*. The tags, or specific descriptors of classroom practice, were grouped into categories or themes that we discussed and refined over the life span of the project. Themes included student support, learning environment, instructional design, challenges in instruction, and instructional evaluation. Tags within those themes included, for example, accessibility, community building, contextualization, metacognition, and baseline of student knowledge.

Over time we created a shared archive of lessons and activities that matched the tags. As a result, when I thought I needed to deepen my feedback on student essays I could go to the archive, which is called Pathfinder, and find great examples of colleagues' strategies for providing commentary. By searching for the term *feedback*, I found examples of effective and efficient ways to provide formative comments that were priceless. For example, one faculty member created a rubric aligned with the assignment specifications and then checked mastery levels for each specification. Another used Jing software to record his comments as he read an essay, so the student could view the Jing presentation and hear the instructor's comments in context. Using Pathfinder, I finally had a catalog of handouts and strategies that supported my teaching in a very relevant way that were vetted by people whose work I'd observed.

What I learned about myself as a teacher and what I needed to learn to be a more effective one, I learned from my pattern. When I received the colorful pie chart of my teaching pattern, I was chastened because while my pattern indicated I focused on higher order thinking skills, it also indicated that I did little assessment of those skills in the lesson. In other words, I was teaching the difficult skills of critical analysis but not checking to determine if the students understood the process. My mandates for the next semester thus became clear: I needed to include more classroom assessment techniques during each class, more formative assessment, and not assume that the final summative essay would indicate mastery of the skills.

My reflective practice became not only descriptive but also generative. The routine of carefully recording the events of a lesson on a weekly basis, the expectation that my online post would be read, and the structure of the reflection on the class itself as well as the collegial feedback given together provided a deep record of my teaching. More important, it also began to shape my teaching because I became more aware of what I was doing and more able to identify what I should be doing to create more opportunities for student success. Because the routine was, well, so routine, it became part of my planning. It provided a blueprint for my growth as a teacher.

The GSCC tools and routines did have real impact on my own teaching, but the project itself had a broader impact on our collective pedagogy. Because we were 26 faculty in developmental education nationwide, we could get a sense of the different approaches and curricula in our disciplines. As a result, we noted and talked about the great variety of entry points into our courses. This was most apparent in English. Some of us began teaching composition at the sentence level and then progressed to structured essays. Others taught writing as an integrated process. Some of us used rhetorical modes to scaffold writing, others used textual evidence to support the discussion. We finally had a national perspective on what we taught, and we were amazed at the range in approaches to presenting the concepts in our fields. This prompted healthy conversations about curriculum design and also heightened our awareness about the diversity of student populations, needs, and learning styles in developmental education. This was valuable insight indeed.

One might imagine that the depth of reflection, the cycles of comment and response, and the weekly timeline might be a lot of work. That was in

fact our reality. We did juggle teaching loads, real life, and the practice of
GSCC with varying success over the course of the project. Still, most of us
agreed the payoff was worth it. We became fully alive as teachers, aware of
what we were doing and able to identify specific areas for our own growth.
The tools and routines prompted us to think more deeply about each lesson, and we used the faculty archives to find activities and approaches that
engaged our students. Most important, we were part of a community of
passionate scholars, and this generated the energy to persevere. We helped
each other through difficult student interactions, provided sounding boards
for new teaching approaches, and collaborated on curriculum design. The
most amazing thing was that this energy and connection came from our
virtual world because we were teaching anywhere from Hawai'i to North
Carolina, from Michigan to Texas. Although we were not meeting face-to-
face, we were digitally connected by our shared endeavor and by our passion
for teaching students.

As I now move on from a career of teaching, first in a suburban junior
high school and then in a multicultural community college, I'm happy to
pass the torch to our daughter who is the fifth-generation teacher in our family. Interestingly, she graduated from a credentialing program whose focus is
described as reflective practice and systemic inquiry for learning throughout
the student's career. While such metacognition is commonplace and frequent
in education programs, it is rare in real practice because of the intense time
pressures and program demands in the typical educator's reality. Yet at their
graduation, these fledgling teachers spoke passionately about the ways reflection and collegial conversation had enriched their teaching lives, and they
remained committed to maintaining that as they entered their own classrooms. They quoted one of their adviser's mantras, "Stop and reflect and
reflect *again!*" and one of her cautions, "If you think you've got it, then I'm
worried!" as reminders that effective teaching practice is iterative in its best
moments. One of the commencement speakers, a program director, reiter-
ated the essential nature of reflection to effective teaching by retelling an
African folktale in which the wise man says, "You must slow down and let
your soul catch up!"

As a seasoned teacher, I learned via GSCC that when I stop and let my
pedagogical soul catch up, I'm a better teacher because I reflect on what
worked, and more important, what didn't, and I can adjust and adapt for the
next class. The model that has grown out of the GSCC project provides the
structure and the tools for this new and amazing generation of teachers just
as it does for those of us with many years in the field.

From a one-room schoolhouse in nineteenth-century rural Minnesota to
a smart classroom in Silicon Valley in the twenty-first, the four generations

of teachers in my family have certainly encountered a range of teaching environments, expectations, and exigencies. But at the core, the essential element is the same: teaching is a relationship that engages the teacher, the student, and the concepts in a reciprocal and sometimes maddeningly recursive process of learning.

Learning at its deepest is relational. Given any new concept, we ask, What is this like? What do I already know about this idea? How is this information relevant to the world I live in or to what I want to do? And necessarily, then, if the learners ask these questions, the teachers do too, so that teaching becomes ever more authentic as it probes the relationship among students, texts, and the teachers themselves.

My life as a teacher has been a long and fulfilling one, made so by the mentors who guided my early career, the colleagues who shaped my thinking, and most surely by Team GSCC, whose dedication, energy, humor, and expertise infused my final teaching years. The tools and routines of the project, the reflective practice, and the shared commitment to student success deepened the experience. I'd always argued that teaching was a leap of faith, that we really never knew what impact we had on our students or how we affected their lives. The GSCC professional development model seemed to make the unknown knowable and connected me to a community of smart, funny, compassionate, and dedicated teachers. Unlike my great-grandmother, a teacher who taught in an isolated one-room schoolhouse, I became part of a collaborative team that spanned the nation—a classroom without walls.

What an adventure that has been.

Rosemary Arca
English professor (retired)
Foothill College, California

PREFACE

I have worked in community colleges for almost my whole professional career, and I am a proud graduate of Jamestown Community College in my hometown in New York. I have seen extraordinary students who, were it not for community college, would never have had the money, time, or secondary training necessary to achieve a degree. I think of students like Deirdre, growing up in public housing, whose family life was marred by her parents' drug use and who has had times of homelessness in her young life. Deirdre started working in a hair salon to support her son after graduation from high school, watching jealously as the sons and daughters of her customers went to college. Someone at the salon told her she might be able to afford LaGuardia Community College. She enrolled while working full-time, only to suffer kidney failure her first semester. A stroke of incredible luck in the national donor lottery brought her a new kidney, and she began college in earnest, this time as an honors student. Deirdre was the valedictorian and received a full scholarship to Smith, one of the prestigious Seven Sisters colleges. She and her son will never be homeless again.

I think of Aaron, the proud son of a two-parent working-class family who graduated from high school and entered the Marines. His tour of Iraq completed, all he wanted was to find the quickest way to get a professional job so that as a single father he could support his child. He enrolled in LaGuardia's physical therapy assistant program because he knew that starting salaries were about $43,000 in New York, which was enough to pay rent. Inducted into the honors program, Aaron took classes in philosophy, English literature, and business administration. He raised his sights, got a scholarship to Syracuse University, and is now working in communications for a large corporation in New York City. Deirdre's and Aaron's transformations are what give meaning and purpose to my professional life.

But what has tortured me throughout my career are our failures. At LaGuardia Community College, like most large urban institutions, more than 80% of our students come to us with high school degrees but lack the high-school-level skills that are the prerequisites of college level work. It may be the result of poor secondary preparation or the students' less-than-stellar efforts in high school. Or it may be because the students are older and they took math too long ago to remember how to solve a linear equation in algebra. Many of our students do not speak English as their first language, so writing a paper using the subjunctive mood eludes them. And most students are poor, without the familial, social, and experiential base that gives them a sense of why college is important. Because they are poor, they often work full-time at low-wage jobs (or at multiple part-time jobs), taking time away from their studies. They are plagued by all the external conditions of living in poverty in a city—violence, mental illness, drug addiction, and inadequate housing.

Each year at LaGuardia, we enroll more than 4,000 new students, 3,200 of whom need at least one course in developmental language or mathematics skills to be successful in college. At our current pass rates, 1,536 students will not pass those courses.

It is this cohort of students that haunts me: single mothers, unemployed construction workers, youths just out of high school who always passed their high school classes, and immigrants who came to America to escape horrible living conditions and prospects. These students have gone through the bureaucratic headache that is the registration process we require. They have filled out forms, completed financial aid applications, taken placement tests, come to orientation, and arranged babysitting and job schedules to accommodate their classes. They have read syllabi, ridden the subway and buses to come to campus, met with professors, done their homework, attended tutoring sessions, and logged on to Web-based support programs. Some have tried very hard. Some have not tried very hard at all because the habits they learned in other educational settings reward passivity and showing up as adequate levels of effort. Or perhaps during the semester their personal life intervened when a friend or family member died, was jailed, became ill, or they simply lost the belief in themselves and their own agency to succeed in college.

From my fifth-floor office I imagine those 1,536 students forming a line stretching down the sidewalk flanking Thomson Avenue. It's a busy thoroughfare, rife with trucks and police cars with flashing lights, underneath the elevated subway most of them rode to come to class. I think of what won't happen in their lives because we could not help them learn what they needed to learn. And I resolve, again and again, to link arms once more with the extraordinary faculty who go into our classrooms year after year with the hope of making a miracle happen, challenging all the forces that stack up against those 1,536 students who so want a college education even if they might not know how to obtain one.

When we succeed with these students, their lives change forever. At LaGuardia, students who do pass their developmental classes graduate at the same rate as students who entered needing no remediation. But those 1,536 students each semester who fail developmental education face a very different

future. Their family well-being, their community viability, and their participation in all this American life has to offer are curtailed. Very few muster
the courage to try again. Failing a developmental course (or, more likely,
dropping out of a class instead of failing) confirms for these students what
so many educational institutions have implicitly communicated—that they
are not worthy.

Yet an interesting fact emerges when we look at individual faculty members. Some of them, teaching the same classes to the same kinds of students,
do much better than others at helping students learn. I have evaluated hundreds of faculty in my long community college career, and I have witnessed
inspired teaching by amazing faculty. As I enter the last phase of my career,
I desperately want to find a way to support the professional development of
all faculty who teach the hardest to serve. I want every one of our students
to end up a Deirdre or an Aaron—achieving against all odds, climbing from
poverty into the middle class, and realizing their greatest aspirations.

It is the desire to support faculty that led to the creation of Global Skills
for College Completion, a research and demonstration project we describe
in this book, and *Taking College Teaching Seriously: Pedagogy Matters!* is a way
for us to share our thinking and detail how to help college faculty improve
their own teaching so that more students succeed. As this project unfolded,
my faith in the expertise, scholarship, and commitment of college faculty
has been reaffirmed. *Taking College Teaching Seriously: Pedagogy Matters!* was
written to not only challenge college faculty but also acknowledge and celebrate their incredible work every day in our colleges' classrooms.

Gail Mellow
President
LaGuardia Community College, New York

SCOPE OF THE BOOK

Why is college teaching so important now? What is the reality of college teaching? What are the unseen and unheard challenges faculty face? How do we document and name the parts of pedagogy that have long seemed invisible? At the heart of this book's inquiry are faculty at community colleges, institutions that have received increased attention in recent years on issues of policy, curriculum, and funding. More than 50% of undergraduates in the United States attend community colleges. By many measures, particularly college completion, America's undergraduate education is underperforming. This is vitally important in community colleges, because America's future goes to college here. Many issues confront community colleges working to help students get to the finish line of graduation—curricular design, advising and student support, financial aid, job placement—and many initiatives have begun to address the set of complex variables that have an impact on the graduation rate of low-income students, notably those who are first in their families to attend college. However, too little attention has been paid to zeroing in on teaching and its corollary, learning.

In the pages that follow, we describe a reflective practice process for college professors that enables them to examine and improve their pedagogy. The introduction discusses the challenges of American higher education, what the research tells us about teaching and learning, and what faculty members need in order to improve their effectiveness in the classroom. From there, we outline the framework and history of our model and the goals we seek urgently to achieve. Chapter 1 underscores the complexity and value of reflection for improving teaching practices, the tools of technology, and the benefits of online communities in creating open spaces for dialogue. In Chapter 2 we walk the reader through the theory of change that undergirds our professional development design. In Chapter 3 we name the tools and routines of faculty engagement, using many examples, to show what this work looks like. Chapters 4 and 5 discuss in detail the infrastructure of the project's online community, with a focus on the interpersonal and technological dimensions. Finally, in Chapter 6 we reflect on the work accomplished so far and issue a call to action to engage faculty in the multifaceted process of reflection, adaptation, assessment, and improvement.

Ultimately, this book reflects on reflecting. The wisdom of such an approach lies in the following: Studies of college teaching have so often fallen short because there is no common language to discuss obstacles. Additionally, most professional development does not occur within the context of practice. We present a model that meets these challenges head-on to great effect.

We wrote this book because we believe our students need *all* possible avenues of support to achieve the ever more essential certification of higher education. Among these, none is more pivotal to student success than the relationship with and effectiveness of individual faculty. We also wrote this to honor the extraordinary teaching that happens day after day in classrooms around the country. Now is the time to bring faculty back into focus as the United States seeks to increase graduation rates of the students of this new century.

INTRODUCTION
Pedagogy and American Higher Education

In the eyes of most faculty members in research universities, teaching is an art that is either too simple to require formal preparation, too personal to be taught to others, or too innate to be conveyed to anyone lacking the necessary gift. (Bok, 2006)

Our aim in this book is to outline a sustainable, cost-effective way to support faculty who want to improve college teaching.

We are all too aware that some faculty members, particularly those in research universities, disdain undergraduate teaching. This can be seen even in the language used to describe college teaching; faculty refer to teaching *loads* and research *practice* with the connotation of teaching as heavy and research as the true professional activity. We argue that this orientation should not be considered standard or even modal. Most college faculty are invested in teaching and many engage fully, taking pride and care in their practice. And most, we believe, are interested in professional development that would help them to improve their teaching so more students learn and succeed.

In this introduction, we outline the research basis and the development process we used for the professional development model we describe in the coming chapters. We begin with a historical review that suggests why college teaching has been neither carefully examined nor valued. We then look at why attention to teaching might be critical at this juncture in time, particularly as we in the United States seek to increase the portion of the labor force that has the skills and income derived from a college degree and, in the process, to educate the new majority students (students of color, immigrants, part-time and older students, and first-generation college students).

The students of today bring a host of complex issues into a college learning environment, issues that faculty may not have had to face previously and that reflect a student experience quite different from the faculty members'

1

own educational and experiential backgrounds. We review the literature on what is known about the nature and the impact of college pedagogy on student achievement, outlining why, despite good evidence about effective college pedagogy, it is infrequently implemented across colleges. Box A provides one faculty member's lament about the lack of honest feedback most college professors receive about teaching.

We argue that pedagogy is an underexamined element of higher education. Colleges are set up to place far greater emphasis on *what* is taught than *how* faculty members teach it. Members of college faculty senates might argue endlessly about which topics should constitute an institution's general education requirement but not utter a word on *how* those topics should be presented.

Academic history is telling when examining why colleges do not place more emphasis on the quality of teaching. College culture evolves from an assumption that faculty members are a group of brilliant iconoclasts who need total freedom to pursue and instill knowledge. It is why stories of completing a class with the gruffest, most obtuse, and most unapproachable professor become a badge of honor, not a sign of inadequate teaching. This is not to say that faculty seek to make it difficult for students to learn; however, there is too often a gap between what faculty intend and indeed believe they are doing and what students perceive and are actually learning (Ratcliff, Jones, Guthrie, & Oehler, 1991).

Box A College Teaching as a Solo Practice

The only time someone else comes into my class is when I get observed by the dean once a year. Occasionally I will have a guest speaker or someone from advising or something like that, but they rarely give me feedback, especially something that could be seen as critical. When I was a long-term part-timer, I was observed twice—in 10 years—zero feedback, zero growth. If this is the experience of the average part-timer, who teach 75% of our classes, that is something to think about.

Christopher Watson, mathematics faculty, Bunker Hill Community College, Massachusetts

---

What Impedes a Focus on College Teaching?

The agreement of 45 states to identify a set of K–12 common learning objectives is unlikely to happen in higher education (National Governors Association Center for Best Practices & the Council of Chief State School Officers, 2010). The broad array of college discipline areas and the speed with which research findings push disciplinary boundaries result in constant changes in curricula, mitigating proscriptive teaching practices, even within disciplines. Higher education elevates content knowledge above all, and institutional reward structures confirm this. Colleges recruit, hire, and promote based almost exclusively on degree attainment and subject matter knowledge, de-emphasizing the skill of undergraduate teaching (Halpern, 1994). The faculty member who is teaching the least is often of higher status and paid more than those whose focus is on teaching (Halpern, 1994). Evaluation of faculty teaching remains a blunt instrument, limited to student satisfaction surveys and the untrained peer observer (Kember & Leung, 2009). On the other hand, the magnitude of teaching demands is also a factor in understanding the amount of time faculty possess to reflect on their teaching (Twombly & Townsend, 2008). Realistic images of faculty range from the wizened professor relying on yellowed lecture notes and mumbling the same lecture once a week to a community college English professor teaching five classes of 35 students each, grading five papers for each student each semester, and providing advisement and curriculum development on top of all of that teaching. Knowing what college faculty actually do is at the heart of the issue of the quality of college teaching and why an improvement process of any kind must be realistically embedded in the context of how each professor's teaching is organized.

The culture of colleges tends to reify faculty independence. This stems in part from the huge variety of disciplines represented on a campus and the lack of sharing across fields but is also rooted in a historical preoccupation with academic freedom (Shaffer, 2011). Faculty independence and autonomy sustain a closed-door orientation in classroom teaching, with faculty possessing a keen sense of ownership over their teaching methods and materials. A downside of the relentless focus on independence can be isolation among faculty, with few viable avenues of support in advancing teaching expertise. The high value placed on independence may explain why the literature is rife with faculty refusing to participate in administration-led projects, particularly those with activities that proscribe teaching practices (Tagg, 2012).

For the economic or academic elite, the quality of college teaching may be irrelevant. Some of the literature even suggests that by the time students enroll in an Ivy League college, college itself has a rather minimal impact on their intellectual development (Pascarella & Terenzeni, 2005). Judging by the low persistence and completion rates among less advantaged students, we cannot assume this is the case for them. They lack the academic resiliency to succeed in spite of weak teaching. The perceived irrelevancy of college teaching stands in sharp contrast to K–12 teachers who must complete a specific education curriculum, participate in a teaching internship, and pass a certifying examination. College administrators, in effect, presume that if faculty members know a topic, they can teach it well enough, and their students are talented enough to learn.

What Is It About the American Undergraduate That Increases the Importance of Teaching?

The oft-repeated but nonetheless compelling assertion that a college degree for the twenty-first century is what a high school degree was for the twentieth century has meant that the number of individuals going to college in the United States climbed to more than 18 million undergraduates in 2012 (National Center for Education Statistics [NCES], 2013). This number undercounts community college students who are seeking a degree by more than 60% because the federal government uses outdated assumptions and counts only students who enroll full-time, for the first time, and in the fall semester (Cook, 2011). The students who go to college today are vastly different from the students who attended college even 20 years ago. The majority commute to campus (Karp, Hughes, & O'Gara, 2010), attend part-time (NCES, 2013), work (Survey, 2011), and are female and 25 years or older (NCES, 2013).[1] While most full-time first-year students are traditional-age youths who have just graduated from high school, the configuration of part-time students is more heavily nontraditional. Student enrollment from all racial and ethnic categories has increased in the past 30 years. Black and Latino students are most likely to attend community colleges (Century Foundation, 2013), and the gap in graduation rates for racial and ethnic groups of students remains stubbornly large (Bowen, Chingos, & McPherson, 2009). Indeed, the data become starker when examined by type of higher education institution. For example, 58% of students attending community colleges are from the bottom 50% of income levels in the United States, compared to 15% at highly selective colleges (Century Foundation, 2013). Sixty-two percent of community college students attend part-time, and more than 56% work more than 20 hours a week (Porchea, Allen, & Phelps, 2010), compared with four-year colleges, where less than 22% are part-time and 24% work more than 20 hours (NCES, 2013). The variation in student profiles contributes to vastly different teaching contexts for faculty, which in turn makes the assessment of the quality of teaching even more complex (Clouder, Broughan, Jewell, & Steventon, 2012). Certainly there appears to be a strong connection between the financial context of a college (percentage of full-time faculty, amount of support services provided to students, tuition, and percentage of students from privileged backgrounds) and the ability to consistently offer a high-quality college experience (Devlina & Samarawickremab, 2010).

While the popular media often depict college students as athletes or entrepreneurs happily attached to the distractions of technology (D'Antonio, Barnhardt, & Greto, 2013), far too little attention is paid to the challenges of poverty, mental illness, poor health, criminal involvement, attention deficit disorders, or homelessness, let alone the interaction among these factors, as aspects of college student life. Because students with these challenges are represented on college campuses in large numbers, they raise issues for administrators and present challenges for faculty. Faculty descriptions of students in their classes demonstrate just how diverse, complex, and challenging teaching in higher education is today, as illustrated in Box B.

The high failure and dropout rates of American students in higher education tell us that many parts of the system are themselves failing. Teaching may not have been a professional priority historically, but in our search for a more educated population we cannot afford to ignore so obvious a component of the learning equation. Indeed, our research and experience suggest that most faculty are hungry for professional support to help them better ensure the success of their students. Until now, the opportunities to secure this support have been scarce, underfunded, undervalued, and, we would argue, ill-conceived.

Box B   Faculty Face Complex Student Issues

Attendance continues to dwindle. I contacted the mother of my mother-daughter students who had missed two classes. She told me that her son had just been sentenced to 25 years to life plus 10 years for aggravating circumstances, and that her mind was not on school. Instead, she intended to get a job and support him any way she could. After all the rhetoric I gave her about how staying in school and getting a higher-paying job would help her more, and so on, she told me she understood, and appreciated my calling, but that her first priority was not on school. This came the same week as another student e-mailed me that her grandmother had a stroke and that she was the only person who could take care of her. What can I do? The importance of writing an essay pales in comparison.
Robin Ozz, Phoenix Community College, Arizona

The third student . . . has done very well but then missed three days. She e-mailed me back and let me know that she was put in jail for the past three days because she forgot to call her probation officer while she was out shopping on Black Friday. She has three DWIs and is trying to change her life. She will be in class today.

Terry Shamblin, Monroe Community College, New York

Two students did not bring their copies of the book, and one student reported that she had tried to read the book and didn't understand a word of it. I hope she's overstating the situation, but I am worried. She's a student who has exhibited several signs of emotional difficulties earlier. When I told her her grade would be lowered a couple of points because her paper had been turned in late, she burst into tears and insisted that my policy "wasn't fair." When I was talking to another student after class, she interrupted us several times and insisted that I talk to her first. I feel unprepared to handle her situation . . . even though I don't yet understand what it is.

Peter Adams, Community College of Baltimore County, Maryland

The ones struggling are the students who are having a hard time staying focused for more than five minutes (literally). I worked with about half the room before we went over the answers collectively and did some of the examples on the board. I have to be intentional in attending to all the students. I can easily be focused on this group who are disruptive and unfocused (when they have my attention, they will work and try, but as soon as I move to the next person, they are unfocused—really I have not seen a class like this maybe ever).

Kate Smith, Monroe Community College, New York

What Does Research on Pedagogy in Higher Education Tell Us?

While research is a fundamental part of what higher education institutions do, it is unusual for professors to look at their own profession as a legitimate topic of study. The late Ernest Boyer (1990) proposed that the scholarship of teaching is sufficiently important to be separated from the scholarship of discovery. Boyer sought to bring greater institutional recognition to teaching, suggesting that excellent teaching is marked by "the same habits of mind that characterize other types of scholarly work" (p. 11). His work is widely read but has had negligible systemic influence in higher education.

Defining *College Pedagogy*

College pedagogy, like most complex and dynamic practices, is not easily defined. Often there is no definition, leading one scholar to note, "An elaborate personal belief system among teachers arises out of the many uncertainties endemic to classroom teaching. In a landscape without bearings, teachers create and internalize their own maps " (Kagan, 1992, p. 65). Andre Pollard's (2010) definition of *pedagogy* is useful: "Pedagogy is the practice of teaching framed and informed by a shared and structured body of knowledge" (p. 7). Pollard's emphasis on practice, a structured body of knowledge (knowledge of *how* to teach and knowledge of *what* to teach), and the need for a *shared* knowledge base are particularly noteworthy.

Diana Laurillard (2002) defines *teaching* as interactive and iterative, and the *learning process* as a dynamic set of relational activities by teachers and learners that cycles between theory and practice. In the complex reality of a learning environment, the practice of teaching and learning occurs between the instructor (which could be a book, a website, or a person) and learner and among the learners themselves, and it embodies the different pedagogical approaches of didactics, social constructivism, constructionism, and collaboration (Mellow, Woolis, & Laurillard, 2011). Although Laurillard's work is not yet widely used in practice, we find it heuristic, agreeing with her that faculty agency in improving their own teaching is fundamental to any practice improvement process.

The Research Literature on College Pedagogy

A 20-year review of articles published in the journal *College Teaching* and the series *New Directions for Teaching and Learning* catalogs an active body of research and innovation in college teaching methods (Mellow, 2013). These are generally accounts by faculty of their own practice in different teaching modalities (active learning, cooperative learning, problem-based learning, multidisciplinary approaches, technology-assisted learning, and discipline-specific learning). The articles' authors also look at specific student learning assessment processes, analyze different theoretical perspectives on learning, examine the work of different kinds of faculty (adjuncts, teaching assistants, new PhDs), and consider how different learning environments might be suited to different kinds of students.

These descriptive contributions by individuals or teams of faculty are taken a step further in environments of supported dialogue and interaction. This occurs in the United States most often at conventions of national organizations. Conveners over the last several decades have included the now (sadly) defunct American Association for Higher Education, the Carnegie Academy for the Scholarship of Teaching and Learning project, the Association of American Colleges & Universities (AAC&U), the League for Innovation, the National Institute for Staff and Organizational

Development, and a handful of smaller initiatives (Hutchings, 1993). Their shared focus is on multiple ways to encourage faculty to engage with one another in discussions of teaching, such as creating course portfolios (Hutchings, 1998), working across disciplines to help students integrate knowledge (Huber & Hutchings, 2005), using case studies of teaching as models (Hutchings, 1998), or creating focused faculty discussion on pedagogy (Mentkowski et al., 2000).

A further advance in connecting ideas to action occurs locally in campus-based centers for teaching and learning. Often led by faculty, these centers have enjoyed a loose relationship with the overall quality of teaching on a campus since the early 1970s (Rouseff-Baker, 2002). The impetus for these teaching centers has been varied. Some support new PhDs who lack teaching experience, some support teaching assistants, and others are comprehensive programs that include orientation for new faculty and extensive workshops covering a variety of pedagogical issues (Lieberman, 2005). However, few centers support adjunct faculty who now constitute almost half of the teaching force in higher education and the majority of community college faculty. Whatever the audience, center administrators can find it difficult to engage faculty in changing pedagogy because there are few incentives to reveal problems or seek solutions (D'Avanzo, 2009).

It is still the case, however, that much of the analysis of college teaching boils down to endless suggestions about how to use what other faculty have used, usually as examples of one theoretical perspective or another. Reading journals such as *College Teaching* will always prove fruitful for the faculty member who is exploring ways to improve his or her teaching. But any one article, for example, on how to use formative assessment to improve student learning, devolves into something inquisitive readers might or might not use, without any sense of how the technique might fit them, or whether it is the kind of change that would deepen or expand the faculty member's ability to teach well (Fluckiger, 2010). Broader analyses of college teaching, such as Matlin's (2002) analysis of cognitive psychology as applied to college teaching, are instructive but hard for an individual faculty member to fully embrace—where would he or she start? How much of what a professor currently does has already incorporated elements of the cognitive science of learning?

Although research from the 1990s reviews pedagogy as a proxy expression of power relations in the classroom (Giroux, 1991; Kanpol, 1992; Luke & Luke, 1990; Tompkins, 1990), most research on pedagogy describes a single kind of pedagogical activity across disciplines or a specific approach to teaching topics within a specific discipline (e.g., Bierman, Ciner, Lauer-Glebov, Rutz, & Savina, 2005; Garner, 2006; McKlenney, 2006; Perin, 2000; Summers, Beretvas, Svinicki, & Gorin, 2005). More rarely, research on college teaching might evaluate the comparative value of a teaching methodology, such as the comparison between teaching a massive open online course and a traditional class (Johnson et al., 2013; Mullins, 2013).

Any focus on pedagogy in higher education, limited though it has been, can be traced to the pioneering work of Arthur Chickering and Zelda Gamson (1991). Their "Seven Principles for Good Practice in Undergraduate Education," published shortly after Boyer's (1990) seminal work and still widely cited (a search in Google Scholar reveals more than 5,000 citations in 2013), places practice into the lexicon of college teaching and codifies what college professors should do to promote learning in their classrooms.

The seven principles characterize good teaching as marked by ample contact between faculty and students, cooperation among students themselves, and active learning in which students participate through activities such as problem-based inquiry, collaborative projects, and public demonstrations of their learning. The principles encourage faculty to hold high expectations for student learning, provide prompt feedback to students, allow for the diverse talents students may bring to a subject, and provide multiple ways of learning the content. Finally, according to Chickering and Gamson (1991), good undergraduate teaching requires students to spend significant time on a task as a way to short-circuit such common college activities as cramming for a test. The principles were established primarily through a literature review and validated by surveys of faculty and an inventory of faculty practices at the time (Chickering & Gamson, 1987; Chickering & Reisser, 1993; Johnson Foundation, 1989a, 1989b).

Recent trends in research on college teaching reflect the continuing influence of Chickering and Gamson's (1987) work, now employing the more generic terminology of *high-impact practices* with reference to activities in and outside the classroom (AAC&U, 2007; Brownell & Swaner, 2009; Kuh, 2007, 2008, 2009; National Survey of Student Engagement, 2013). High-impact practices generally ask more of faculty because these practices are likely to involve students in collaborative instruction, academic activities that occur outside the classroom, and a more thoughtful and individualized assessment process for the work students produce (Kuh, 2009).

The majority of research on high-impact practices examines college teaching on a small scale in a specific discipline, usually in a particular geographic setting at an individual college. For example, research might examine how to use an inquiry-based teaching method in science (Fayer, Zalud, Baron, Anderson, & Duggan, 2011), how to help students connect their educational experiences across disciplinary boundaries (Bass, 2012b), or how to phase multiple writing assignments in college English (Haswell, 2008; Riehlea &Weinera, 2013).

Large-scale survey instruments have been developed based on high-impact practice research, using self-reports from students or faculty as a proxy for quality instruction. These data, accumulated over time, have been used to encourage adoption of improved higher education practices (e.g., www.ccsse .org/aboutccsse/aboutccsse.cfm; http://nsse.iub.edu/html/about.cfm). Overall, a significant body of research affirms that engaged pedagogy has a positive impact on students' learning, ranging from general intellectual competencies and critical thinking to moral development and persistence in college (for a comprehensive review of the latest literature, see Trowler, 2010).

What Do Faculty Need to Improve Teaching?

This review of the literature, particularly Chickering and Gamson (1987) and its offshoots, makes clear that many teaching methods appear to be superior approaches to college teaching, but too few faculty members are using them. The problem in supporting pedagogical improvement among college faculty is as much about finding ways to encourage changes in practices as it is about needing to create new ways to improve. It seems clear that those in higher education (and perhaps all education) are more adept at proffering ideas than effectively implementing those ideas.

The failure to implement ideas effectively suggests that the powerful intrinsic motivation that faculty possess to help their students succeed is not being tapped. This is in part because the strategies offered to improve college teaching frequently overemphasize the descriptively didactic ("Do these things") and underemphasize the professional evolution that might occur with an iterative and thoughtful reflection on practice, the reverse of the approach encouraged by Laurillard's (Mellow, Woolis, & Laurillard, 2011) interactive and iterative depiction of the college classroom.

The distinctive power of American higher education comes in no small part from faculty who are given the freedom to structure what occurs in a college classroom, leading to multiple authentic, open-ended, and creative approaches that keep the teacher and those taught interesting and interested. The tools we describe in the pedagogy matters practice improvement model are beginning steps toward a network of engaged faculty who work together to educate the next generation of college students.

Origins of the Model

A welcome focus on community colleges in the United States has emerged over the past five to seven years, with large investments from the federal government and philanthropies such as the Lumina Foundation (primarily through the Achieving the Dream project), the Bill & Melinda Gates Foundation (in a variety of national projects), The William and Flora Hewlett Foundation, the Carnegie Corporation of New York, and The Kresge Foundation. Most of the investments made individually and collectively have focused on reform of curricular structures, student support services, and policies affecting persistence and completion, most notably public college reimbursement formulas and student financial aid. Many promising practices are emerging from these investments. Yet, what we have not seen is a focus on pedagogy and the teaching support college faculty require in order to improve their impact on student persistence and completion.

The pedagogy matters practice improvement model has roots in work begun in 2010 with funding from the Bill & Melinda Gates Foundation. The premise of the original work was that among the initiatives aimed at improving community college student persistence and completion, none focused on *pedagogy*—the impact of the professor in the classroom. The principal investigators theorized that teaching, as differentiated from subject matter expertise, *had* to have an effect on student outcomes just as, if not more, significant than the impact of data-driven student advising, integrated academic support programs, and reformed financial aid policies. This, we reasoned, would be particularly true for the poorest and least prepared students—the majority of those assigned to developmental education.[2]

Why pursue this hypothesis beyond an intuitive presumption? Because there is ample evidence of the impact of teaching and teachers in the K–12 environment. How can the teacher be the most important contributor to student learning for an 18-year-old and not be for an 18.5-year-old or for a 45-year-old for that matter, particularly a student who lacks self-confidence and has difficulty mastering the foundational knowledge and skills deemed necessary for success in college-level work?

Our work began with a focus on faculty at U.S. community colleges—those who teach more than 50% of all undergraduates in the country. It homed in on faculty in developmental mathematics and English; that is, those who teach students who have graduated from high school but who do not exhibit the high-school-level academic skills necessary to succeed in college courses. As Yarnall, Gallagher, Fusco, Remold, Schank, Feng, . . . and Tidwell-Morgan (2010) write,

> It really cannot be emphasized enough that perhaps no other cohort of instructors in American education confronts such a consistently low-performing group of students on a daily basis. At almost every other educational level, classrooms represent a mix of students, both those who excel and struggle with school. At selective 4-year universities, professors

interact almost exclusively with a subset of students who have "survived" and excelled in education. In such settings, the distinction between "weaker" and "stronger" students is so fine as to be an almost superfluous consideration. In the everyday life of a classroom, each competent and engaged student provides a sense of mental respite for the teacher, while each struggling student requires additional focus and effort, and no small measure of self-questioning, as the teacher grapples with the question, "Why doesn't this student understand?" This ongoing triage and self-questioning process is compounded as the number of struggling students in a classroom increases.

In focusing on faculty members teaching the hardest-to-serve students, we sought to develop a model that would support them in improving their practice and also be an important contribution to the broader higher education profession.

The Problem

Community colleges in the United States are the most underfunded sector in higher education, usually receiving less support per student than elementary schools. With the smallest amount of funding per student, community colleges serve the poorest, most at-risk college students (see Figure I.1), which is almost synonymous with serving students of color because community colleges draw from specific geographic communities that tend to be stratified by race and class, particularly in urban settings.

These facts lead to two critical challenges. The first is that poor students tend to have an inadequate high school education, which leads to high rates of placement in developmental education—close to 90% at most urban community colleges. The second is that inadequate funding has caused community colleges across the country to depend on adjunct faculty to teach developmental education courses while making it impossible to provide them with sufficient professional support to craft effective teaching strategies for this very complex student population. It should be noted that the dependency on and lack of professional support for adjunct faculty members goes beyond developmental education because adjunct faculty members now teach the majority of community college students.

Our Focus

In a Jam, an asynchronous moderated and structured online exchange with more than 800 full-time and adjunct faculty, participants estimated that teaching accounts for about *one third* of student success. While we do not have

Figure I.1   Socioeconomic Distribution at Colleges by Selectivity, 2006

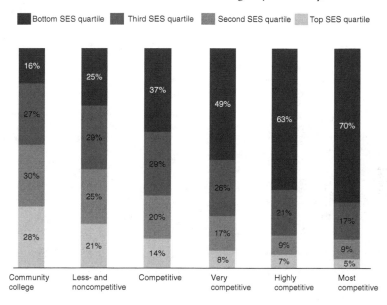

■ Bottom SES quartile   ■ Third SES quartile   ■ Second SES quartile   ▨ Top SES quartile

Note. SES = socioeconomic status. Some columns do not total 100 because of rounding. From "How Increasing College Access Is Increasing Inequality, and What to Do About It," by A. P. Carnevale & J. Strohl, p. 137, Figure 3.7, in R. D. Kahlenberg (Ed.), *Rewarding Strivers: Helping Low-Income Students Succeed in College*, 2010, New York, NY: Century Foundation Press. Copyright 2010 by the Century Foundation. Adapted with permission.

an independently verified assessment of the impact of good teaching at the college level, we do know that a good teacher in K–12 has enormous influence. Effective teachers can advance a K–12 student the equivalent of a full grade level (Hattie & Marsh, 1996). It seems reasonable then to think that the same is true in college, especially in colleges that serve at-risk students. We believe the time is right and the need is compelling to increase our return on the human capital assets of systems of higher education in the United States by focusing intensely on supporting faculty in improving their personal pedagogical skills.

If pedagogy does account for 33% of student success, anything we can do to improve in this sphere will only add to the impact of actions in curriculum, student support policies, and so forth. As practitioners, we are seeking actions that are practical and can be implemented on the ground at a manageable cost. We have all been involved in wonderful projects that are very successful but whose cost is high. In New York's lauded Accelerated Study in Associate Programs, students who receive financial support and intensive academic advising and coaching graduate at much higher rates than their peers—but at an additional cost of $4,800 per student. At LaGuardia

Community College (LaGCC), where Gail Mellow is president, to give all incoming freshman this wonderful program would cost $16 million annually. We must find a way to support teaching excellence that is effective and sustainable.

Here is what we estimate. There are about 8 million students in community colleges in the United States, 60% of whom (at a minimum), or 4.8 million, need developmental education. If these students are distributed on average into classes of 28 students, then roughly 125,500 developmental education classes are offered each semester throughout the country. If 60% of the classes are taught by adjuncts (a low estimate), then about 110,000 adjuncts teach these classes (less if they teach more than one class), and about 7,500 full-time faculty members probably teach the remainder, if we estimate that each full-time person teaches two classes on average. At current average pass rates for students in developmental education, if each of these instructors was able to help just two more students per class succeed, pass rates would go up 7%; four more students would push rates up by 14%, which would allow 672,000 people to take a huge step toward graduation.

The Work: Understanding Pedagogy

The frame for the initial work funded by the Bill & Melinda Gates Foundation, originally known as Global Skills for College Completion (GSCC), was an action research project. The goal was for those leading GSCC to work closely with a group of exceptional community college faculty from across the country. Our objective was, using the particular attributes and benefits of technology, to document and analyze the pedagogical practices of these exceptional faculty and at the same time help them reach two more students in their classes. As a result of this collaborative work, we developed the pedagogy matters practice improvement model, a set of what we call *tools* and *routines* that focus on supporting faculty in improving their teaching. As far as we know, it is unique on several counts. First, it emerged from the engagement, observation, and assessment of the work of outstandingly successful pedagogues. Second, the experience is integrated with actual teaching and involves self-reflection and peer exchange, critical elements of adult learning and behavioral change. Third, it is designed to be scaled organically but exponentially at an affordable cost.

We write this book with a larger hope, however. We believe that focusing on faculty practice improvement is critically important to groups of faculty far beyond those who teach developmental education. In this book, we summarize what we have learned about college teaching, faculty engagement, and the ways technology can support thousands of college faculty who are facing students who must make it through college but who are not like the students who have sat in colleges in times past.

How We Got Here

The research and development project GSCC, which is the base of the pedagogy matters practice improvement model, used the intellectual prowess and on-the-ground application experience of two national cohorts of faculty, one working over four semesters and one working over two semesters, to delve into the process of how to support good teaching in practice. We used online technologies to help us understand what highly effective college developmental mathematics and English professors do in the classroom.

Gail Mellow, president of LaGCC, and Diana Woolis, founding partner of Knowledge in the Public Interest, are the two principal investigators who, along with Gerardo de los Santos, president of the League for Innovation, submitted the original proposal for GSCC. We believe the strength of the design is in part because of this unusual academic, nonprofit, private partnership. The LaGCC team managed the project and served as the subject matter experts and the voice of the academy; the Knowledge in the Public Interest team developed the online strategy, managed the online engagement of faculty, and designed and supported the technology while working closely with the LaGCC team to continually modify the tools and routines of the project. The League for Innovation led involvement with the larger field of community colleges, particularly by featuring the project at several conferences. During the work of the first cohort of faculty, this core team was joined by SRI International, led by Louise Yarnall, as the external evaluator.

However, ultimately it was the faculty who gave shape and substance to the project. The initial group of math and English full-time faculty were nominated by their college presidents and invited to apply to be included in faculty Cohort 1. Twenty-four faculty members from across the country were selected based in large part on their high pass rate records.[3] The goal was to bring together this outstandingly successful group of teachers (12 math and 12 English) from 16 states and 18 colleges to deconstruct the elements of their pedagogy. We assumed we could use this knowledge to define the *best* developmental education pedagogy, but we were dead wrong. What we discovered was much more complex and nuanced. We found that the best faculty members use a range of strategies to reach the students in their classes.

We created an online process that allowed us to observe these great faculty members in action and for them to observe each other. Each participant chose one of the developmental classes he or she was teaching as a focal point. Faculty members kept an active online professional journal of all class activities, posted student work and three videos of themselves teaching, and wrote reflections on their sense of how and why each session of the chosen class went well or poorly. In addition, the instructors interacted with one another periodically in structured sessions aimed at identifying the best ways to teach developmental students.

All the faculty reflections and student work were captured digitally. We used the volume of digital data as the basis for a qualitative analysis. With SRI, the external evaluators, we created and validated a set of authoritative pedagogic categories derived from practice in the field. We used these categories as digital *tags*, or descriptive labels, inviting instructors to highlight and tag their own work in subsequent semesters, with what we found to be high rates of interrater reliability. As instructors tagged their work, the tags became a powerful common language of the details of teaching practices, and they became another data set. Gathered as frequency graphs, we found we were able to use the tags as data points to form a pedagogical pattern for each professor's teaching practice.

We used our findings to create an online prototype that served as a platform for a second national group of 24 faculty who undertook further testing and refinement of the practices developed with Cohort 1. Cohort 2 members were still volunteers but with average student pass rates. Twenty-five percent of the Cohort 2 members were adjuncts. We employed four faculty members from Cohort 1 as online coaches, taking over the role previously played by the project team.

Changes in student achievement in both cohorts are promising, affecting retention (keeping a student through an entire semester) and pass rates with differences ranging from 4% to 8% improvement (see Figure I.2). Of greatest interest is the improvement among students of adjunct professors, 14% to 15%, albeit with a very small sample.

Why We Write Now

If GSCC and the model it spawned engaged faculty but did not affect persistence and success, it would not warrant further development. However, sustaining an educational reform without strong faculty engagement is impossible. In our case, the level and intensity of engagement and the faculty's embrace of the process were beyond anything we had expected. Indeed, the external qualitative evaluator for the second GSCC faculty cohort, SPEC Associates, produced a rubric that validates very high rates of engagement

Figure I.2   Mathematics and English Retention and Pass Rate Changes for Cohort 1 and Cohort 2 Compared to Nonparticipating Faculty

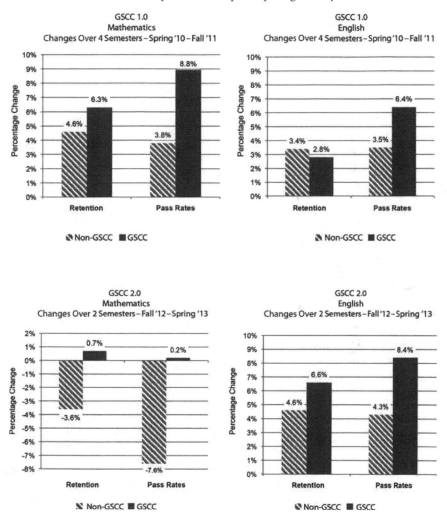

Note. GSCC = Global Skills for College Completion.

and, more important, professional growth connected to engagement. It is this combination of highly engaged faculty working through a process that leads to improved student outcomes that has prompted our writing this book. We believe that we have created a new way to use technology to support instructors in improving their teaching. Two participants summarize their experience in the following way:

Participating in [the project] this year has helped me to be more reflective in every single action. I constantly analyze how each session went. . . . [It] gave me the tools to think about every minute detail of a classroom. Tagging the lessons helped me to see how each choice, action, and event had a purpose and role in the students' success. I truly believe (and hope) that this reflective action will follow me for the rest of my teaching career. (Misty Evans, English professor, Murray State University, Kentucky)

I think the continual self-evaluation and reflection allowed us to work together to brainstorm improvements and positive tweaks to be more purposeful in our classrooms as opposed to just randomly reaching in the dark for ideas and techniques in *hope* of success. (Claudia Delgado, mathematics professor, Hudson Community College, New Jersey)

So we write this book to share what we have learned about the process of supporting the deep and important work of faculty practice improvement. As the title of Norton Grubb's (1999) book states, college teaching is honored but invisible. In this book, we make the case for why pedagogy matters to colleges and to the ultimate success of their students. We also make the case for why supporting college faculty to improve their craft is a key missing element in raising graduation rates in American colleges and why making teaching visible is so important.

Our work has given us the space and the time to explore teaching at community colleges across the United States in great detail. What we have found more often than not is a treasure trove of incredible faculty, anxious and willing to adapt and adopt new strategies in their teaching if it will help their students learn, but adrift when it comes to knowing what to change and how to do it in practice. The reflective and dialogic practice we outline in the following chapters shows faculty in action and highlights the scholar practitioner's honest struggle with students who arrive in class with poor academic preparation and whose education is often disrupted by the injustices and indignities of poverty and the hard realities of family, work, and health that are ever hovering.

Our goal is to articulate a vision of faculty leading a professional development practice that causes students to learn more and engages faculty deeply in the scholarship of teaching in order to continually improve their practice. We write this book humbly acknowledging the arduous challenge so many faculty take on, year in and year out, to help their students learn. In every way, we write this book to assert that pedagogy matters!

Notes

1. Almost a third of part-time students work 35 or more hours a week, although this number has decreased slightly over the past decade (NCES, 2013).
2. We use the term *developmental education* throughout. Synonyms are *basic skills* and *remedial education*.
3. Neither course content nor assessment is uniform among community colleges. Consequently, the selection criterion was faculty who were in the top 10% in pass rates on their campus or in their system.

1

The Contours of Practice Improvement

Americans have spoken with their feet by enrolling in ever-growing numbers in institutions of higher education. They are responding to the opportunities of an economy that needs them, in turn, to succeed by acquiring the habits of mind and the skills to participate in it fully. The majority of these students confound the stereotype of an undergraduate as a full-time and fully supported learner. Rather, they attend school while also working, commute to campus, and skew above the traditional college age range of 18 to 21 years old. Administrators of institutions of higher learning have been experimenting with and investing in ways to support the evolving student body. However, none has figured out how to solve the challenges of low persistence and completion.

The factors that drive any one student to drop a class, fail a class, or leave school are complex and specific to that person. It is, however, possible, and even probable if the student is the first in the family to attend college, that he or she has been overwhelmed in trying to negotiate the college's administrative structure and has failed to make connections with instructors, leading the student to feel they have no choices. The professoriate is underprepared for the challenges these students present but is by no means indifferent to their fates. In our experience, professors care a great deal about their teaching and want their students to learn. What they won't do is compromise their gauges of learning and understanding in order to move along an unprepared student.

Countering the isolation of traditional teaching and helping faculty members help more students succeed is our mission. Because higher education lacks compelling models, we have looked afield for inspiration and guidance. Three domains—adult learning, computational social science, and communities of practice—give shape to the core of our work. We have applied elements drawn from these fields with research on and experience with technological applications. It is this combination that has enabled the most innovative aspects of our approach to practice and practice improvement—the tools and routines of the pedagogy matters practice improvement model.

The Knowns of Adult Learning in the Workplace

Adults learn best when the topic has import and immediacy; that is, it is something they are working through in a real-life situation. Lave and Wenger (1991) coined the term *situated learning*, which takes place in the same context in which it is applied. In general, situated learning is most successful when it occurs within a community of like or similar participants who cocreate learning objectives, discuss and use examples from their own work rather than textbooks or training manuals, and are able to ground their learning in their own experiences.

The Power of Reflection: What? So What? What Now?

Since at least 1933 with the publication of John Dewey's (1910) *How We Think*, Donald Schön's (1983) *The Reflective Practitioner: How Professionals Think In Action,* and Nona Lyons's (2010) *Handbook of Reflection and Reflective Inquiry: Mapping a Way of Knowing for Professional Reflective Inquiry,* the process of reflection has been identified as central to professional learning. According to Schön (1987), reflection is understood as having two time horizons: "reflection-in-action" or the kind of artistry that good teachers use in everyday work in the moment and "reflection-on-action," looking back to something we did to better understand the outcomes of our actions (p. 26).

In the reflective process the person doing the reflecting, or the learner, is involved in the following stages of inquiry:

- Description of the experience: What happened (the basic facts of the experience under consideration)?
- Analysis of the experience: Why did this happen, how does the person feel about it, what did he or she learn?
- Critical action: What will he or she do as a consequence, how does this insight inform the person's future action (Brookfield, 1995; Mezirow, 1990)?

Carol Rodgers (2002) gives substance and shape to the term *reflection* and its specific application to the professional development of those who teach. She notes with regard to *reflection* that "without a clear definition it is difficult to research the effects of teacher professional education" (p. 842). Indeed, her distillation of Dewey's work has provided clear guidelines and benchmarks for the pedagogy matters model. According to Rodgers:

1. Reflection is a meaning-making process that moves a learner from one experience into the next with deeper understanding of its relationship with and connections to other experiences and ideas. It is the thread that makes continuity of learning possible, and ensures the progress of the individual and, ultimately, a social group of the field.
2. Reflection is a systematic, rigorous, disciplined way of thinking, with its roots in scientific inquiry.
3. Reflection needs to happen in community, in interaction with others.
4. Reflection requires attitudes that value the personal and intellectual growth of oneself and others. (p. 845)

The pedagogy matters practice improvement model is thus anchored by the concept of reflection and designed to support a reflective practice that is dialectical, experimental, and collaborative. In a pedagogy matters community, faculty are action researchers and as such act together, collectively examining particular challenges identified by individual community members. Because the model capitalizes on technology, the individual and collective reflective processes are captured digitally. This digital record generates important data that become part of the reflective process, thus reinforcing a cycle of deep learning, grounded in authentic experience, that yields insight the learner and the community can use to take action.

Social Affordances and Platform Design

If the literature of adult and professional learning tells us that we must give faculty members the chance to integrate the experience of teaching with the opportunity to reflect on this experience, alone and in collaboration with peers, the feasibility of such a construct, operationally and financially, begs the incorporation of technology. Indeed, it is the combination of ease of access, ease of use, and purpose-built design provided by technology that makes possible the pedagogy matters revolution in professional development.

The design of the pedagogy matters platform draws on work called *social affordances,* which refers to activities made possible by technology. Sun and Chen's (2014) framework offers four dimensions of affordances: social connection, information aggregation, reflection and expression, and dialogue and collaboration. In the pedagogy matters practice improvement model we expand these to specifically address collaborative learning, the cocreation of new knowledge, and analytics. Sun and Chen's description of social affordances is one of many (e.g., see Ellison, Weber, & Gibbs, 2013; Gruzd, Haythornthwaite, Paulin, Absar, & Huggett, 2014; Tess, 2013; Wagner, Vollmar, & Wagner, 2014). This body of work has allowed us to select and incorporate the ideas and insights about platform design that seem to speak most directly to engaging faculty in examining and assessing practice and improving student outcomes.

Inspiration and Aspiration: Computational Social Science

Computational social science enables the observation and empirical study of phenomena. As an instrument-based science, the instruments take the form of computer systems that interrogate large data sets using algorithms to detect patterns and represent them visually. This makes possible the rendering of otherwise invisible subject matter or the explication of relationships that would otherwise not be observable or understood (Cioffi-Revilla, 2010).

The analysis of large data sets can stand in for or supplement third-party observation or experimentation. Deriving knowledge from computational data is enhanced by visualization because the pictures drawn by the data are organic, not subject to preconceived ideas about relationships among specific variables.

While the application of computational social science to interactions among people is seen more often in the algorithms that run Google than in educational research, computational social science has begun to be applied to a range of human interactional data. It has been used to provide insight into questions such as how productivity is affected by social networks, how happiness can be mapped over a 20-year period, and how disease, smoking, or obesity spreads among groups (see Lazer et al., 2009, for an overview). Lazer and colleagues have even examined how collecting large amounts of human interactional data and mining it for patterns could form a path to understanding the human interactions that are a part of the teaching-learning cycle (Lazer et al., 2009).

It is difficult to capture, let alone coherently categorize, what teaching *looks like* over an entire semester, valuable as this would be to any instructor. Nonetheless, with the assets of technology it is possible to do in some form and, in developing the pedagogy matters practice improvement model platform, computational social science led to a design that allows us to quantify and make visual the rich digital record of reflective practice for each instructor, as it is recorded and debated over successive teaching periods.

Indeed, the payoff for incorporating a computational social science approach into the pedagogy matters practice improvement model is in pattern visualization. The conversion of human interactional data into patterns that can be represented graphically holds enormous power to provide insight, provoke reflection, and give structure to discussion. Our goal is to enable a professor to see, understand, and work with his or her personal pedagogical pattern and, over time, to facilitate the analysis of the patterns of thousands upon thousands of professors to see what we can come to understand more deeply about effective teaching and learning.

Adoption and Adaptation: Communities of Practice

While computational social science has provided the methodology for gathering the data of classroom interactions, the field of communities of practice has helped us fashion the environment that engages faculty and, in effect, generates the data. This element is critical to pedagogical practice improvement because historically faculty have not been provided the structures to engage with one another over the practice of teaching. Indeed, the New Media Consortium (2013) and EDUCAUSE identify the difficulty in scaling teaching innovations as one of the key (negative) trends in higher education. As an example of the challenge, one Florida community college was a pioneering participant and leader in the development of a new curriculum and pedagogy for developmental mathematics (Clyburn, 2013). This college not only participated in the first flight of experimenting colleges but also supplied faculty leadership for the national initiative. The initial results showing improved student achievement were solid and exciting (Clyburn, 2013). Yet some of the college's developmental math faculty refused to participate in the work, and faculty resistance mounted to such an extent that the faculty became unwilling to participate in the second round of the project (Fong, 2014).

Communities of practice are organizational structures that have been successful in supporting innovation and adaptation at scale (Hildreth, 2004). A community of practice is a group of individuals with shared professional interests and expertise. The community is designed to provide interaction, problem solving, and resource sharing, thereby enabling the participants to advance their understanding of a topic and incorporate the new knowledge into their work. Communities of practice allow participants to collaborate and support one another with a goal of deepening professional understanding and creating the context for the social development of new knowledge. A pioneering voice in the field is Etienne Wenger (1998), who began observing naturally occurring groups and has launched, studied, and advanced methods to foster effective communities (Wenger-Trayner & Wenger-Trayner, 2014). Community designs, although increasingly incorporated as an essential part of innovation and practice in business, are only beginning to make their way into the academy (Owyang, 2008).

As communities of practice have evolved, they have become synonymous with online communities of practice because technology enables a dispersed group of people to remain in close touch over an extended period of time. Successful online communities are created when the community

- forms a collective identity;
- articulates a clear purpose;
- incorporates effective moderation;
- structures a clear and easy process for sharing knowledge and expertise;
- establishes guidelines for participation;
- maintains a highly usable way to have social interactions, and, perhaps most important;
- measures the success of the community in creating change among its participants (Athey, 2001; Booth, 2011; Cambridge, Kaplan, & Suter, 2005; Fini, 2008; Owyang, 2008).

Goal-driven online professional communities work best when their purpose addresses real-life issues, what Knowledge in the Public Interest (Fontaine, 2002) terms a *point of passion* or *point of pain* (Woolis, 2014). By doing so, the participants return again and again because the community of practice is of value to them. Effective online professional communities are grounded in work, making collaboration essential and productive, and they have clear metrics to assess the perceived value of group work to the individual community members (Foroughi, 2011; New Media Consortium, 2013; Woolis & Restler, 2014). Early research suggests that professional development conducted through an online community of practice results in changes to how teachers teach (Farooq et al., 2009; Laksova, Mann, & Dahlgren, 2008; Laurillard & Masterman, 2010).

Communities of practice can leverage the collective intelligence of the group by carefully building assessment and analysis into the community in an iterative and dynamic way so that knowledge is extracted from the work itself and is used to refine the routines inside the community (Woolis & Restler, 2014). The most effective communities make sharing new knowledge an ongoing part of the interaction, using facilitation, moderation, curation, and analysis, embedded in the ongoing work of the community, to support innovation in practice (Barker, 2005; Keitt, 2011; Woolis & Restler, 2014; York, 2011). At its best, an online community of practice is also sustainable at scale, provided that the process of expansion is thoughtfully structured, the issues being worked on continue to deeply interest participants, and the environment continues to be engaging, challenging, and supportive (Woolis & Restler, 2014).

Assessing Engagement

If the degree of engagement is the essential measure of an effective professional practice community, then it is necessary to assess and evaluate the quality of the engagement in any community. The pedagogy matters practice improvement model uses an engagement rubric designed by SPEC Associates, a nonprofit research and evaluation group, to monitor the quality of faculty engagement (see Box C). The concept of deep self-reflection, which is determined by whether a faculty participant considers why or how something is important to student success and therefore deserves consideration, is the core of the rubric. The hierarchy of deep self-reflection values self-reflection over general reflection as an indication of professional growth. The rubric encompasses five levels of sequential progress. It can be applied to faculty narratives and reflections, moving from description (Level 1), to reflection on why the practice is important (Level 2), to statements of intention of changing a particular practice (Level 3), to changing to a broader approach to teaching (Level 4), and finally to changing to an approach based on evidence that it helped students learn (Level 5).

Open Space

Open space for dialogue is an important part of a community. It is a counterweight to the dominant characteristics of a vital and productive community of practice—the structured and assessable interactions. In an open space the personal and the professional can mix, as they do in the offline world around the proverbial water cooler. It is conversational exchanges of this nature that contribute to the personal connections that build engagement. In the pedagogy matters practice improvement model this online space is called the *coffee klatch*. It is the virtual faculty lounge of the community. It is an unstructured online space available 24 hours a day, seven days a week for any posting and dialogue on any and all issues, professional and personal.

The pedagogy matters practice improvement platform and the routines of the pedagogy matters practice improvement model described in the chapters that follow draw on the domains of adult learning, computational social

Box C Rubric to Assess Faculty Engagement

Level	Explanation	Examples

Level 0
Appreciation
Logistics
Administration
	Entry is general or vague with respect to classroom practice or approach to teaching:
	• Most entries coded at this level are in response to another post
	  They often express polite to enthusiastic appreciation but no other thoughts about the nature, implementation, or rationale for a particular practice or approach
	• Entry addresses anything other than classroom teaching, including
	  • logistics related to participation in the project (Polilogue, Classroom Notebook, Coaching Circles),
	  • administrative issues at the faculty member's institution, or
	  • personal (versus professional) comments
		"Great job!"
		
		"Thanks for the suggestion. I'll definitely try that in my class!"
		
		"That's interesting."
		
		"Would someone explain the difference between the tags for Variety in Presenting Information and Differentiated Instruction?"
		
		"Have fun with your families over the holidays!"

Level 1 Description	Entry is nominal or descriptive: • Describes what faculty and students did in the classroom • Poses general questions about classroom practices or teaching approach • Lists changes made in practices or approach without explanation of why changes were made • Describes how members felt about a class without discussing what they did or why they did it • Suggests the use of alternate practices or approaches without explanation of why they are relevant or appropriate.	"The lesson covered the influence of a, h, and k in the quadratic function $f(x)=a(x-h)^2+K$ as an introduction to completing the square to transform a function into this form."

(*Continues*)

Box C (*Continued*)

Level	Explanation	Examples
Level 2 Reflection	Entry describes a particular teaching technique or approach to teaching AND shows evidence of analysis or reflection about why to use this technique or approach. For example: • Why it mattered for students • What they learned about their students or how to teach them effectively In the case of reflections about one's peers, entries explicitly recognized what the instructor is doing and why. They may also: • Thoughtfully relate other practices or knowledge to what is observed in their peers' specific practices or general approach, and/or • Ask thoughtful questions to better understand what the instructor has done and why he or she did it.	"For this lesson, I started with a review of key concepts that included an informal assessment of students' understanding of quadratic functions. I wanted to be sure they were ready to move on to the next level—completing the square of a quadratic function. Otherwise, they would get frustrated and I'd just be wasting my time!"
Level 3 Change in classroom practices (either planned or implemented)	Entry lists, names, or describes: • Plans to change or adopt specific *classroom teaching practices* (e.g., techniques, activities, assignments) • Changes in classroom practices that have already been made • Why changes will be (or were) made	"When reviewing material, I usually just ask for a show of hands to find out who gets it. But this doesn't always work, and sometimes I'm moving ahead when I should still be reviewing. So next semester I'm going to start using the clickers our department purchased to have students answer review questions anonymously and get a more accurate read on the percent of students who are ready to move on."

Level 4 Change in approach to teaching (either planned or implemented)	Entry lists, names, or describes • Plans to adopt *"best practice" approaches to teaching* developmental students, • Changes in approach to teaching that have already been made, AND • Conveys why changes will be made	"When looking at other people's tags of my lessons, I was surprised to not see more tags for challenging instruction. But I can see now that a lot of activities and assignments ask them to do kind of mid-level thinking, maybe applying skills but not comparing how they are used in different situations and getting them to construct general rules for when to use different skills. So over the summer I'm going to look at my lesson plans and see where I can add some more critical thinking kinds of activities, so I can challenge them more."
Level 5 Change in approach to teaching (implemented/impact observed)	Entry lists, names, or describes changes that have already been implemented in their approach to teaching developmental students. AND Entry clearly relates changes in approach to teaching to OBSERVED impact on students—either informal observation or formal assessment of academic or nonacademic outcomes.	"I used to think I did a good job of getting my students to think critically. But I hadn't really considered getting them to think about how well they were learning through different types of activities. I started doing more of this at about midsemester and have been amazed at how thoughtful it has made them be about the content as well as their own learning styles. I still have some more thinking to do about adding metacognition to lessons I'll teach next year, but I think it's totally worth the time to do it."

science, and communities of practice for their broad frame and structure. This is not, however, a static model. The very nature of this way of working necessarily requires adaptation—the incorporation of new elements and the refinement of others. This is partly because, if the model is to have utility, it must have the capacity to adapt to different contexts. Equally important, it must respond to the accumulation of data born of use. Another vital and valuable stimulant to adaptation is the ever-changing landscape of social technologies, which have increasingly rendered human interactions easier and richer. We remain alert for those affordances that support collaborative reflective practice, that are consonant with faculty culture, can be embedded in work, and facilitate the collection and assessment of evidence.

2

Theory of Change

The theory of change that undergirds the model we offer here is based on a standard change cycle of *plan, do, reflect, act,* with the foundational tenet that professional practice improvement requires the capacity for self-reflection. Our theory of change assumes that a faculty member who is open to change, willing to engage in a dialogue with other professionals, able to integrate new strategies into ongoing practice, and motivated to use the information derived from practice as the basis for further inquiry is most likely to change his or her teaching successfully. Thus our change theory conceives of the first step as mindfulness, when a professor becomes more focused and aware of his or her own actions and the actions of others in the teaching process (see Figure 2.1). The second step creates a level of metaperspective as the professor labels and categorizes key elements of his or her teaching practice. The third step is to become more intentional about the connection between actions in class and student responses to the actions at an appropriately granular level.[1] This leads to the fourth, and perhaps most challenging, step in which the faculty member tries to change an action in the classroom that represents an innovation, adoption, or adaptation of a teaching strategy. The faculty member iterates this process and evaluates the impact of the change in practice on student learning, reflecting on his or her own actions and engaging in inquiry with others. We believe that the opportunity to repeat these steps in the community over time and with students in the classroom leads to profound and positive changes in teaching.

Figure 2.1   Reflective Pedagogy Practice Improvement Cycle

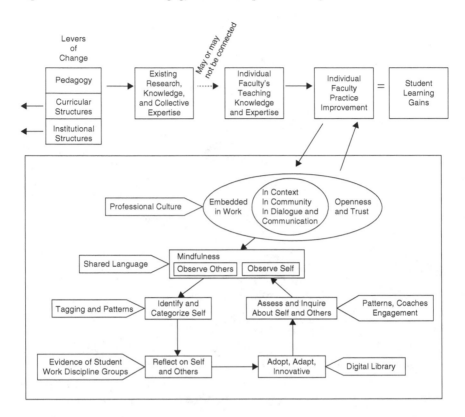

The Five Critical Elements of a Pedagogical Practice Improvement Model

The literature on adult learning theory, social affordances of technology, computational social science, and online communities of practice constitute the foundational input for the pedagogical practice improvement model that is reflected in this theory of change. However, the theory of change and the conceptual model we present here also reflect the contributions of the two cohorts of faculty we worked with as action research partners as part of the GSCC project described in the introduction. Indeed, it is because of their collective contribution and that of our evaluation partners that we have the confidence and drive to share the work.

The model we present in this book and reflect in this theory of change rests on five elements that we have come to understand are absolutely vital to an effective practice improvement process for faculty in higher education:

1. Faculty learning *reflects academic culture.*
2. Professional learning is *embedded in work.*
3. Effective learning about one's pedagogy is *backed by evidence* of personal engagement, changes in practice, and improvement in student learning.
4. Professional learning generates and uses data to *make teaching visible.*
5. The practice improvement process *leverages the social affordances* of technology to build community, establish a common cultural milieu and language, and share and build professional knowledge.

Our theory of change acknowledges that college teaching is one of at least three major elements in the academic ecosphere that ultimately affect student learning success. The other two, institutional structures (e.g., advising systems and financial support) and curricular structures (e.g., prerequisites and course alignment) are often hard to move and are regulated in some way. Only pedagogy is (mostly) controlled by individual faculty behind closed classroom doors. Pedagogy is the one thing faculty can self-regulate, even when they are given a curriculum and told how to teach it.

Obviously no one currently teaching in higher education is a tabula rasa from a pedagogical standpoint. Faculty work within a realm of *existing knowledge and collective expertise.* The following is an example of how Peter Adams, an English professor at Baltimore County Community College, Maryland, gives context to his teaching:

> Early on, I was much affected by the work of Sandra Perl, Nancy Sommers, and Flower and Hayes, and I continue to use their ideas about writing processes to inform the way I organize my courses, with a lot of attention to pre-writing and even more to revision. In fact, for the first paper each semester, my students do a lot of brainstorming and short writing to move them toward an idea they want to write about. And they revise their first paper a minimum of four times, often more, in response to suggestions I make.

Even more of everyday practice, however, is born of accumulated teaching experience. A math professor at Patrick Henry Community College in Virginia provides the following description of a useful tool invented by Bronte Miller, also a math professor at Patrick Henry:

> One of my favorite (and easiest) mechanisms to encourage connections in class starts on the first day of the semester. I give my students paper clocks and tell them that they must go around the room and make twelve appointments with twelve different classmates. When they make an appointment, I have them each share something about themselves. For example, I might tell them that they must tell each other their favorite flavor of ice cream.

I make the students keep their clocks all semester. Almost every day from then on, I come into class, put a time up on the projector and the students must pair up with their appointment for the day. I tell the students to introduce themselves to their partners and tell them something about themselves (like which season of the year is their favorite and why). Then throughout the class period I have activities that students must do with their partners. I love my appointment clocks because every student gets paired with someone different every day, it's a very fast and easy way to get the students paired, and my little "get to know you question" helps the students get acquainted. The pair activities during class also require the students to talk to each other to work out the math. I am always amazed and thrilled by what I overhear the students discuss while in their pairs. They stay on task (for the most part!) and really encourage each other. I hear them making dates to meet in our math lab after class for tutoring. I hear them giving each other tips on how to negotiate our homework software. It's *great*!

In full recognition of the personal and institutional contextual realities each college professor faces, we offer the following description of the five elements that are the foundation of the pedagogy matters practice improvement model.

Reflects Academic Culture

Faculty members are notorious for resisting change. Peter Senge (2006) cautions, however, that resistance should be categorized as not only a force aligned against change but also the energy that is holding the center and therefore the only locus from which to instigate sustained organizational change. This is where most academic change strategies fail, because of a lack of appreciation for the values, habits, and aspirations of an organization (Katzenbach, Steffen, & Kronley, 2012). The literature has many examples of faculty refusing to participate in what are perceived as change processes (Tagg, 2012). In our work we explicitly reject the concept of faculty buy-in because that formulation describes a process whereby a third party creates something, and then the creators attempt to get faculty to buy the idea and implement it with energy and rigor. An effective professional development process is more appropriately animated by perceiving faculty culture as the foundation on which to enact an effective strategy rather than something to be finessed.

The model we describe uses faculty culture as its bedrock. It emphasizes faculty engagement as an expression of professional expertise, uses faculty autonomy as a wellspring of innovative energy, and emphasizes peer review and interaction as the highest form of rigorous improvement coaching.

Strategies that not only appreciate a culture's impact but also strategically employ the culture to advance an aspirational goal can maximize the energy in a system (Senge, 2006). A process for pedagogical improvement must incorporate faculty culture as a positive force for change and do so as flexibly as possible. College teaching is a personal practice, honed by years of experience and guided by disciplinary, institutional, and departmental beliefs. This suggests that the uniqueness of faculty practice ultimately requires an improvement process customized to a market of one. This is not to suggest that all teaching activities are equally effective, but that the professional judgment of faculty about when and where to apply these activities is a critical aspect of moving from theory to practice.

Embedded in Work

A central element of the principles of adult learning is learning gained through self-direction and application. The adult learner often pursues learning for a specific purpose. Most professional development opportunities for college professors are offered at conferences away from the *Sturm und Drang* of the college campus. The approach, even if dialogic, almost never occurs within the context of practice. How often do we hear about a teaching strategy with real promise, close the journal or leave the conference room charged with enthusiasm for change but ultimately implement a pale version of the practice as time intervenes? This is even true of workshops and courses. Most professional development focused on teaching becomes a one-off, a time of interaction with ideas or colleagues that remains largely in the realm of the theoretical.

The close practical guidance embedded in professional development in many other professions, such as the lawyer or the surgeon or the accountant conducting professional work alongside other professionals and where the work itself is examined and explored, has heretofore been off limits to college professors. The hundreds of thousands of college classrooms are closed spaces, with neither a history nor a habit of review focused on professional advancement in teaching.

The practice improvement model we offer capitalizes on technology to enable a faculty member to integrate professional development into a normal workday, infuse practice with reflection, and give autonomy to choose with greater intentionality where and how to improve. Detailed evidence of one's teaching practice reinforces the interplay between theory and practice, between experimentation and refinement, and between the ideal and the all-too-messy reality of a college classroom. It provides a context for the close examination of a specific class of students. Incorporating a professional development process into weekly teaching practice gives a faculty member a new instrument in the arsenal of strategies. In the same way the microscope gave scientists a new perspective on the world, we offer a tool that hands professors information about the interaction between their own actions and student responses, and ultimately opens up new vistas in student learning. Integrating reflective practice into the ongoing flow of a semester makes the tacit explicit and sharpens focus and intentionality in those moments of faculty-student interaction that make a difference.

Backed by Evidence

Most attempts to improve the effectiveness of college as it pertains to college students look at student outcome data. Measures vary and may answer any of a number of questions: Did the student pass the course? Pass a common examination? Stay in college? Pass a national certification examination? Show improvement via a cumulative assessment test such as the Classroom Assessment Scoring System? Transfer grades or find a job in his or her field? In addition to these measures, there is increasing thoughtfulness and thoroughness among some college administrators in the collection and examination of evidence of deeper student learning, such as those who use authentic student work accumulated in ePortfolios for outcome assessments (Arcario, Bret, Klages, & Polnariev, 2013).

We suggest two ways evidence should be used in practice improvement in teaching. First, have a sufficiently detailed common language so that descriptions of what is occurring in the teaching delivery process can be identified. In our work we use a closed authoritative set of tags, or descriptive labels, to provide this. If tagging provides the shared language for substantive dialogue, evidence of student learning provides data points for grounded discussion. Thus, we consider it essential for faculty to use a common language to review and codify what they did in class. Second, secure evidence of actual student work in response to their teaching. Such evidence includes artifacts of student learning as captured in formative assessments via classroom assessment techniques (CATs; Angelo & Cross, 1993), because information on changes in student learning that can be tied to faculty practice can influence adaptation and change in a reflective practice experience. Further, tagging faculty practice provides organization of the content of teaching behaviors and a basis for content curation, which builds the value of the evidence, allowing for synthesis and making the evidence not just searchable but understandable.

Evidence of improvement in faculty teaching, however, is not commonly captured. As Randy Bass (2012a) has noted, researchers are unlikely to attempt to understand how and why something was learned, which is as true for the impact of professional development activities on faculty learning as it is for student learning. In the rare instances where professional development is delivered over several time periods, the element of practice in vivo in which faculty members have tools to watch themselves or one another is rare. With the exception of instances where faculty videotape themselves (usually in a single time frame), there are few instances of faculty having access to data that gives them evidence of their teaching practice.

To be effective, professional development for faculty should make practice improvement changes substantive by collecting evidence of not only a professor's understanding of a pedagogical concept but also how he or she has put that understanding into practice and, most important, how it has worked with his or her teaching style and for his or her students.

Makes Teaching Visible

Faculty members need all the support possible to sort through how and why their teaching strategies help students to learn. Patterns are one strategy to condense multiple sources of data into something humans can comprehend. We focus on patterns because everything that endures through time, space, and context rests on a pattern. We are most familiar with the expressions of patterns, whether it is the pattern of stripes on an animal hide that signals tiger or the data points that express a Mandelbrot fractal. Patterns are ways to abstract and summarize complex input, and visualization of those patterns helps a practitioner understand interactional data. Patterns support faculty understanding of who they are as teachers and offer a way to see their practice in a holistic and detailed manner.

The challenge of identifying causality is made even more complex by the adaptive requirements of college teaching. Diana Laurillard (2008a) has said that college teaching is not rocket science; it is much harder because there is nothing in teaching to rely on as the basis for taking action that parallels, for example, the constancy of the known rules of physics. We find that making practice visible by displaying aggregated pedagogical data in the form of patterns is a potent way for faculty to understand and investigate pedagogy and to customize their change strategies.

Leverages Social Affordances

The importance of community for faculty is evident in the literature (Hutchings, 1998; Hutchings & Schulman, 1999). Practice improvement needs to tap this peer-to-peer aspect of faculty culture. It is a key element of our model and has the ancillary benefits of ensuring scalability and sustainability. The critical requirements of an online professional practice improvement community are e-dialogue, sharing and adapting ideas and materials, and collaborative problem solving among peers. We believe, therefore, that social interaction is foundational to any effective strategy to support college faculty. The interaction, however, must go beyond sharing and occur within a structure that supports a rigorous examination of one's actions, comments by peers, and support to change.

A Word About Technology

Technology makes the model we have developed possible. It is not impossible to record and even tag a lesson reflection and attach a formative assessment off-line, but two critical features are almost impossible to include in an off-line environment. One is peer-to-peer and coach-to-peer commenting, which is necessarily an asynchronous activity each person completes according to his or her personal schedule. The other is the evolving pedagogical pattern, which is automatically recorded and adjusted as the faculty work unfolds over time. As we present the model in the ensuing chapters we explicate the supporting role technology plays in each part of the process.

The pedagogy matters practice improvement model thus attempts to connect several lines of critical inquiry and research. It presumes that professional development for faculty must incorporate adult learning theory, maximize the affordances of technology for social interaction and community building, and rely on new conceptual frameworks that emerge from approaches such as computational social science. The pedagogy matters model builds further by incorporating five foundational elements particularly responsive to college faculty. Namely, the model grows out of a faculty culture that prizes scholarship and autonomy, integrates learning with the work of teaching itself, creates an evidentiary basis through formative assessment, and makes teaching visible to a community of peers who help one another achieve professional improvements. Technology is a thread throughout the theory of change, but basic human parameters of reflection, setting goals, feedback, and experimentation animate the system of professional development and improvement.

Note

1. Laurillard's (2012) conversational framework presents a more complex picture in examining what occurs in a classroom and represents the teacher in dialogue with a learner and each learner in dialogue with other learners and the materials of the class. It is why she says, "College teaching is not rocket science. It is much, much harder" (p. 5).

3

Pedagogy Matters
Tools and Routines

Through a theoretically grounded action research investigation, we have identified the critical elements of an engaging and change-making professional development process. It is only viable because of what is now possible with the benefit of technology. The model we describe here is a first—but we hope important—step in reimagining practice improvement for college teaching. We are confident that the combination of future technological advances and the analysis of experience with the model, accumulated over time, will enable faculty to improve on our process and thereby accelerate and deepen improvements in teaching and learning practices.

The Broad-Brush View

The pedagogy matters model of practice improvement is built using the best understanding we have of adult learning, which we situate in an optimally designed community of practice. The dominant focus is on each individual faculty member because it is his or her work and changed and improved practice, as assessed by the accomplishments of his or her students, that is *the* vital benchmark of this experience. The technology *tool* known as Classroom Notebook, and the activities or *routines* faculty members engage in, are designed to involve faculty in a meaningful but manageable way of recording, reflecting on, and assessing their practice.[1] This emphasis reflects the autonomy of college faculty in general, and specifically as it pertains to their teaching.

Individual faculty member self-reflection is enhanced by a community of peers. Here again, the dominant focus of activity is on one-on-one conversation: giving and receiving feedback entirely focused on specific experiences in specific classes and in specific contexts (student behavior, lesson content, etc.). We believe it is the nonevaluative, structured, and supportive nature of the pedagogy matters practice improvement experience that causes a participating faculty member to choose to become deeply involved in the work.

The bulk of the time spent by a faculty member, and consequently the bulk of the data generated through the use of the pedagogy matters practice improvement model, are consequences of structured and repeated lesson-focused work. This is what allows for the derivation of each person's personal pedagogical pattern, generated electronically in Classroom Notebook. It is the combination of inputs from the teaching pattern and formative assessments of student learning that serve as stimuli for targeted experimentation by faculty. And it is this experimentation that creates the potential for improved student outcomes.

Figure 3.1 is a depiction of the total experience. We discuss each element in detail in this chapter and the two that follow.

Figure 3.1   Diagram of Pedagogy Matters Processes: The Heart of the Work

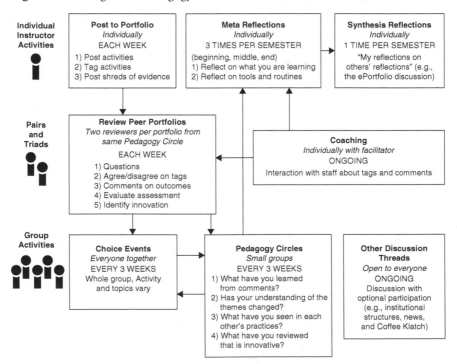

The Heart of the Work: The Routine of Documenting a Lesson

Faculty members select one class that will be the focus of their practice improvement work. They post a weekly record of the lessons of that class on the electronic platform Classroom Notebook, where each person has his or her own space or ePortfolio. In the Classroom Practice section of Classroom Notebook, faculty members follow a template of questions to structure how they write about what happened in class; this is the *routine* for documenting a lesson. The template provides basic comparability of descriptions across faculty and across disciplines. Faculty member online postings give a self-reported detailed view of a particular class, organized by week in the semester—a contextualized, blow-by-blow sense of what is happening in the classroom. They also post all the materials used in the class, including readings, handouts, descriptions of classroom activities, lecture notes, videos or slides, and so forth. As Larry Giddings, developmental English professor at Pikes Peak Community College in Colorado, states

> Attaching prompts, artifacts, and summary notes provide evidence and clarity for what is happening in the classroom. It's an essential point. The artifacts help each of us see concretely the lesson that our colleague described and reflected upon. The artifacts help each of the responders to comment, critique, and reflect as well.[2]

Student data are captured through posting formative assessments and student-produced materials. The depth and quality of the posts and their verisimilitude in evoking the texture of a class is achieved by a combination of guidance from peer coaches and by example among peers.

The power of the simple discipline of documenting one class a week as the basis for reflection is revealed in the faculty's analysis of their work. Most of the elements of the documentation are rare for college professors. Returning again and again to one's own work and the intimate interplay of students, teaching practices, learning goals, and student work makes for a complex self-portrait, challenging faculty to push themselves with greater intentionality as their reflections advance over a semester.

Let's look at an example of the routine of how a faculty member documents a lesson by examining an edited post by Joyce Lindstrom, a developmental math professor at St. Charles Community College in Missouri (see Figure 3.2).

Midway through the spring 2013 semester, Joyce tackled the lesson topic "Rationalizing Denominators, Radical Equations, and the Powers of *i*." In documenting the lesson, Joyce identifies the best thing to happen in class: "Groups of students were able to complete and explain problems for which

Figure 3.2   Classroom Notebook, Classroom Practice

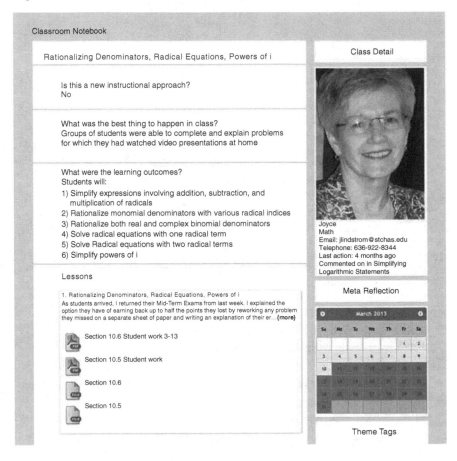

they had watched video presentations at home." For Joyce, who has begun to work with a flipped classroom model, it was a triumph because by the middle of the term students were finally getting the hang of the process.[3] She notes,

> After my frustration last semester of trying to do in two hours what other classes had four to do, I feel like I have found a way to make it work— have the students put in the other two hours at home. While I have explained that expectation before, I had not given the students a specific way to invest those two hours.

What follows is Joyce's description of how she accomplished these tasks in her class period:

> I divided them into groups of three and assigned each group four problems from the departmental notes. Each group completed their problems—with

my assistance as needed—and then each group of three went to the document camera to explain their solutions. (Students are less nervous/intimidated in front of the class and worried that their work is incorrect when they are surrounded by their group mates. While I do not tell them how to divide the presentations, they usually take turns so that everyone who is willing gets a turn.) The rest of the class took notes on each completed problem. I used the students' work to highlight points like rationalizing the cube root in a denominator, not by just repeating the factor that is already there, but by making sure there are three factors under the radical (the "house rules" from Bronte's analogy[4]). We also reviewed in detail the problem with two radicals where isolating one of them gave us a binomial with one rational and one radical term on the other side. From there I led a discussion developing the powers of i and how to simplify them. I especially like the simplification of a negative power of i by multiplying by a form of 1 as a power of i to the fourth power. I emphasized that we have been multiplying by forms of one all semester, but they have always been fractions. Voila! We now have a way to multiply by a power of one that is not a fraction!

To document the work of her students, and thus to assess the impact of her teaching approach, Joyce provides artifacts of the classroom experience. She posts the problems she used as a formative assessment, often termed a *CAT* (after Angelo & Cross, 1993) and attaches to her Notebook scanned copies of students' work that she evaluated as examples of low, middle, and high understanding. Joyce's CAT involved asking students to solve three radical equations at the end of her class period to assess their understanding of the concept and practice. Figure 3.3 shows a student's work Joyce assessed as "high" (although not completely correct) that she scanned and attached to her Notebook.

Figure 3.3   Documenting Student Work in Classroom Notebook

Section 10.6

Solve each radical equation. Remember that the solution is not complete until you have checked each proposed answer in the original equation:

1. $\sqrt{3x+2} = 29$

2. $\sqrt{2x-1} + 5 = 0$

3. $\sqrt{5-x} = x+1$

4. $\sqrt{3x+1} - \sqrt{x+4} = 1$

(*Continues*)

Figure 3.3 (*Continued*)

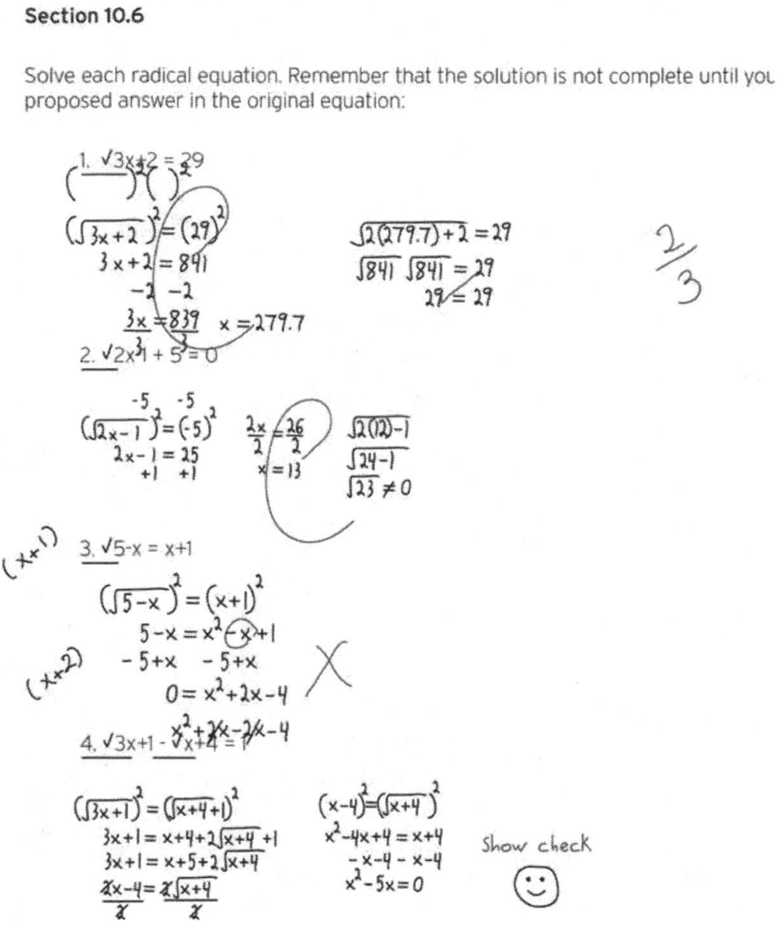
Section 10.6
Solve each radical equation. Remember that the solution is not complete until you
proposed answer in the original equation:
1. √3x+2 = 29
x = 279.7
2. √2x-1 + 5 = 0
3. √5-x = x+1
4. √3x+1 - √x+4 = 1
Show check
2/3

Providing actual examples of student work is a touchstone for colleagues and links teaching approaches at a sufficiently detailed level to allow dialogue about how specific activities in a particular classroom help students learn.

The granularity of the perspective—the ability to see how a faculty member conducts all aspects of his or her teaching—is a window on the classroom that is rarely opened. While some professional development initiatives include class visits or videos, and some colleges use a team-teaching structure, with the benefit of technology the pedagogy matters practice improvement model gives faculty access to multiple instructors and multiple views of their daily teaching practice. The digital capture of the instances of teaching allows peers, and the professors themselves, to return to any lesson and examine different aspects that might become salient over time, particularly when the

Figure 3.4   Overall Reflection in Classroom Notebook

Overall Reflection

1   After my frustration last semester of trying to do in two hours what other classes had four to do, I feel like I have found a way to make it work-have the students put in the other two hours at home. While I have explained that expectation before, I had not given the students a specific way to invest those two hours. While I certainly have much to learn about the flipped classroom, I feel that I have found the tool that will make this doable. Thank you to my Magnificent Math Masters colleagues! During last semester's reviews, questions, and comments, I realized I needed to give the students more responsibility, and the flipped classroom emerges as an option. Whew! The video assessments collected at the beginning of class also provide a way to let students earn credit BY being in class but not FOR being in class.

instructor teaches the same lesson in a subsequent semester. While faculty usually keep mental and written notes of the issues that emerge in their classrooms, a process that captures the class dynamic in a searchable digital mode allows them to do it in a way that won't send them digging through files the next time they prepare to teach the content.

Simply by collecting her work in Classroom Notebook, Joyce is beginning to craft an intentional strategy for what she might change in the next iteration of her class experience. For this, her flipped classroom experiment, she writes the following as a reminder to herself: "It has also been helpful to me to watch all 31 content videos and note that most of them consist of watching the presenter solve problems with very little explanation of the concept behind the solution—a reminder that I need to make certain that the concepts are clear, not just the method." In terms of her pedagogical practice, flipping her classroom is a significant change for Joyce and is the focus of the overall reflection she posts for this lesson in Classroom Notebook (see Figure 3.4). She credits her peer team with helping her arrive at this teaching solution.

The Classroom Practice Template

The documentation of what is happening on a weekly basis in one college classroom is guided by a framework of prompts that set the stage for clarifying goals, describing teaching and reflecting on the teaching-learning experience. The routine of answering the following questions guides the weekly posting in the Classroom Practice section of each faculty member's electronic portfolio on Classroom Notebook:

1. What is your lesson title?
2. Is this a new instructional approach?

3. What was the best thing to happen in class?
4. What were the learning outcomes?
5. How would you describe the lesson (with attachments for handouts, notes, PowerPoint presentations, readings used, etc.)?
6. What is your overall reflection on the lesson?
7. Did you deal with any specific student issues?
8. What assessment(s) did you use (formative and summative, with examples of student work)?

Box D contains an edited example of how Stephanie Fernandes, a developmental mathematics professor at Lewis and Clark Community College in Illinois, answered the first five questions. Her post is from the eleventh week of class, and we include excerpts from each section. The notes in brackets are hot links to the full posting. While the Fernandes narrative is more detailed and extensive than that of most math instructors, it is a fairly standard depiction of the authenticity represented in the weekly postings.

Box D Classroom Practice Template

What is your lesson title? Putting [It] All Together . . . For the Second Time

Is this a new instructional approach? Yes

What was the best thing to happen in class? It might just be the best review day I have ever had.

What were the learning outcomes? Review all the topics in Chapter 3 including: (1) slope, (2) x- and y-intercepts, . . . (6) putting a line in slope-intercept form.

How would you describe the lesson? I began the class by announcing the test for the following class. . . . Our objective today was to go over everything they would face. I handed out index cards and asked the students to write down three challenges they would have to overcome in order to get the grade they want on the test.

What is it and how do you find it? I asked the students to work together to describe six concepts: slope, x-intercept, y-intercept, a solution to an equation, a graph of a line, and an equation of a line. They needed to write a good, simple definition of each term and explain all the ways to determine that piece of information. We completed the first one together to help the students get the hang of it. . . . Students worked together; when they had questions I tried to encourage the students to work it out together. One volunteer, Stephan, went to the board and wrote a great definition for *y-intercept.* He then returned to his seat and announced, "I don't know how to find it." I reminded him that he was not alone; I noted all his classmates who would be willing to help him. I also conveyed my expectation that he finish what he started! . . . Next, I put the test review up and asked the students to complete two questions. I warned them that both were tricky and frequently missed. . . . I allowed them some time to work. . . . We again discussed how to figure out what was going on with the vertical line. I asked what the slope was and they spouted, "It's undefined." I asked, "How could I figure that out if I forget?" We used the definition to work it out. . . . Finally, I picked up the index cards on which the students had listed their challenges. I read some of the challenges. For each, I asked for ideas on rising above that challenge. We discussed word problems, time to study, mixing up topics, silly errors, test anxiety, and others.

 What Is It [PDF of the student index card]

Although all elements of the Classroom Practice routine are important, for many the greatest value is derived from the weekly overall reflection in which a professor steps back from the details of the class and provides a more holistic depiction of why things occurred as they did. This allows the professor to determine the positive and negative aspects of what went on, examining the why and how of student learning in that session. A faculty member might write about how students' actions facilitated or impeded the learning occurring in the lesson, or about an insight into the timing of specific content covered in the semester. The overall reflection provides a chance for faculty to note their insights into their own teaching practice in a particular context during a moment away from the fray, at a distance from the multiringed, action-packed arena of a college classroom. Box E contains an excerpt from Fernandes's overall reflection.

Videos of the Classroom in Action

Faculty also document their teaching by using videos to capture their class, posting three times per semester. Videos can be used productively to verify

> ## Box E Overall Reflection of a Single Class
>
> I will say this was one of the best review days I have ever had as a teacher. I tried to incorporate many of the things that I have been working on.[5] First, I tried to help identify the challenges students are going to encounter this weekend while preparing for the test, and help give some ideas for dealing with them. Over the past few months I have considered the idea that our college students should be responsible and should know how to study. Many are and do, but many are not and don't! So how can I help them? In class, we spent some time discussing study strategies. Honestly, this portion could have gone better. I need to work on the way I conduct this portion of the lesson to make it more personalized and engaging. But I believe that I need time to teach study skills. The next portion of the lesson—What is it and how do you find it—went very well. I was excited by the student's enthusiasm and how the activity pushed them to boil everything down and organize the information. I *loved* how they helped each other and enjoyed each other. . . . In this portion of the lesson my goal was to incorporate group work and challenging tasks. I asked the students to write about the math and I purposely didn't answer many questions directly. I believe in the ability of my students, if I will just get out of the way and let them go. Of course, they will always take the easy way out if I offer it to them, but if I don't most students rise to the challenge beautifully. I also tried to incorporate several different kinds of activities. I wanted the students to feel like this was an essential day to be present. In the past, I have had horrible attendance on review days. I think that just goes to show how ineffectively I was conducting them!

and amplify pedagogical techniques or simply to show the faculty in action, which gives context. Videos convey immediacy in a way that is hard to capture in words and provide the feel of a classroom, an unvarnished sense of the tone and texture of the class—the students, the setting, and the professor are all visible.

Unfortunately, producing videos of college teaching can be a logistical headache. Faculty need to obtain student waivers, position students who refuse to be videoed out of camera range, secure the support of a media tech team, and help the videographer, if there is one, understand whom to video (i.e., don't show the teacher writing at the front of the room while students are doing group work). In general, these homemade videos have terrible sound quality with limited general utility to audiences outside the community of practice.[6]

Nonetheless, we find that even an imperfect recording is highly useful for faculty members and their peer reviewers. "I was struck with how the videos captured the relationships among students and between students and teacher and that can't be replicated with text," said Lori Hirst, English professor at St. Louis Community College in Missouri. Including a video of a class along with the written documentation serves to deepen the interpersonal connection among peers and amplifies (or occasionally contradicts) the self-reported actions of faculty members. Videos can be used by faculty to record their work on specific aspects of their teaching, such as creating a stronger community among students, pushing students toward a greater range of critical thinking, and so on. The video then provides another opportunity for self-reflection and supportive insight from peers.

Because professional development works best with highly engaged faculty, the simple and great appeal of watching one another teach should not be underestimated. When an English professor was despairing over her lesson, a colleague offered the following: "What I saw in your video was you listening, asking questions and allowing the student to work through a hard problem. I was amazed by the ending—the student came up with a good thesis statement by the end of the conversation." There is no doubt that video adds an invaluable dimension to personal and peer understanding of the teaching experience.

Formative Assessments of Student Learning

The Classroom Practice template asks faculty to document their use of formative assessment in each class. Of all the elements of the pedagogy matters model, this is perhaps the one that requires the greatest change of habit for college faculty. Whereas summative assessments are integral to each professor's curriculum—quiz, midterm, paper, final exam—the instructor who regularly assesses whether a specific teaching strategy actually helps students absorb the lessons of a single class is rare. We call formative assessments *shreds of evidence* to convey the idea that they are small and suggestive rather than conclusive input on student learning. They offer feedback to an instructor, raise questions, suggest testable hypotheses, and open an early and easy door to course correction when needed. Indeed, the incorporation of formative assessment into practice is a vital flex point in our theory of change because we have found that the collection of shreds of evidence is a key input for faculty members. It enables them to evaluate the impact of their teaching strategies and—this is important—to be inspired to adopt or adapt new practices to help more students delve into the material and make it their own.

In our work, we draw heavily on Angelo and Cross's (1993) CATs because they offer such a variety of ways to gather data to help faculty determine whether a specific pedagogical technique results in student learning. For example, a formative assessment might tell a math instructor that students appear to understand the concept of equality when solving a linear equation with whole numbers, but they begin to struggle when fractions are part of the equation's solution. Or an English professor might have spent a class on thesis statements and find through a CAT that several students had not understood how to incorporate it except as the opening of an essay. Overall, our message is that data of all kinds are an instructor's friend, and data gathered at the lesson level are very valuable.

Monica Stansberry, an adjunct English professor at El Centro Community College in Texas, describes the value of formative assessment:

> Many instructors underestimate the value of CATs. Several good teachers use CATs in an informal way in the classroom that allows them to check students' progress. Many times these CATs are undocumented and not shared with the students. Providing informal assessments gives students "a sense of mastery each step of the way." This many times gives students more confidence in learning, and it gives them immediate feedback to where their successes and challenges are. In my experience it also enforces learning a new skill. The more the students have practice with the skill, the better they get at it and the more they understand what is expected of them. If an instructor is re-teaching a skill that students have not met, students know they have not met it and, therefore, are more engaged in the lessons that cover their specific objective. Making teachers aware of how to implement CATs in their classrooms make good teachers effective teachers. . . . I now know how to support my intuition that students are learning through the use of CATs. It took a while for me to understand how to insert more formative assessments in my lessons, but I found that slowing down and trying not to infuse too much content at once has helped me tremendously. Now, I am able to focus learning on the troubled spots.

Steve Blount, an English professor at Lewis and Clark Community College in Illinois, notes:

> One area in which I would like to focus next semester is gathering baseline data. One of the lessons I observed this semester focused on the importance of understanding the underlying schema of students' knowledge before tackling the task of teaching. I think that I sometimes assume that I understand what students know when I really am just guessing. Because I am 50 years old and have been trained for years in reading critically, and writing in response to reading, I think that I sometimes forget how young many stu-

dents are and how relatively new this is for them. One of my goals will be to take a closer look at what students know as they enter into my classroom.

Routine: Highlighting and Tagging

Once a faculty member has documented a lesson, we move to the second and vital routine in the pedagogy matters practice improvement model: highlighting and tagging.[7] Using a simple technology-based tool that functions like any highlighting tool for a text document, faculty members identify what they feel is important in their narratives, their materials, and the artifacts of their students' learning. As a consequence of highlighting (literally and figuratively) what they each consider to be the essential parts of their lessons, faculty members become more explicit about why they do what they do in class, more attuned to the evidence of the impact of their choices on student learning, and more deeply reflective about why particular teaching practices are effective.

As stimulating as the process of highlighting is, tagging fires the engine of the pedagogy matters practice improvement model. Tagging—the annotation of highlighted text—is a foundational element of qualitative research and a process used frequently by online writers as a way to create keywords for aggregation of content across multiple postings. In the pedagogy matters practice improvement model, the tags are an authoritative set of knowledge labels that form a higher order classification system that constitutes the model's taxonomy. The tags were derived through a rigorous qualitative analysis of faculty classroom actions (see Appendix A). The tags serve to establish an analytic framework that faculty members use to closely examine their teaching practice. They form the language of Peer Practice Dialogue, and, through tagging, individual teaching patterns are generated. Box F has extracts of faculty descriptions of what was occurring in their class and the specific tag the instructor used to classify their own actions.

The process of highlighting becomes a simple yet highly effective method faculty use to identify important moments in their teaching practice that need to be examined or analyzed. "I find the tags/themes to be extremely useful in reflecting on my own practice and identifying my areas of strength and areas in which I think I can improve," said Kristin Duckworth, Community College of Baltimore County, Maryland. Tagging creates a common language of description at a relatively granular level of analysis for later dialogue. By organizing the highlights into tagged categories, faculty members connect a single action in their teaching to a family of actions. This serves to expand the utility of the highlights from a support

---

Box F   Highlighting and Tagging the Lesson Narrative

The following are examples of tagged highlights.

Text highlighted: "The students worked together; when they had questions, I tried to answer them with leading questions or just encourage the students to work it out together." Tagged as *Peer Engagement*.

Text highlighted: "I noted all his classmates that would be willing to help him. I also conveyed my expectation that he finish what he started! The other students were fantastic. Several worked together to help Stephan finish perfectly." Tagged as *Community Building*

Text highlighted: "I asked the students to work together to describe six concepts: slope, x-intercept, y-intercept, a solution to an equation, a graph of a line, and an equation of a line. They needed to write a good simple definition of each term and explain all the ways to determine that piece of information." Tagged as *Higher Order Thinking*

---

for individual reflection to a structure for a more comprehensive analysis. According to Michelle Zollars of Patrick Henry Community College in Virginia,

> I love the tags and reflection. I can see from tagging where my strengths and, more importantly, my weaknesses are. I can look at my peers and see how they present information in a more effective way than I do. I reflect constantly, always questioning myself on how I can improve. I also have my students reflect more—on classroom information, college life, goals, everything!

Steve Blount, an English professor from Lewis and Clark College in Illinois, wrote,

> When I look at my semester pattern I notice that my highest areas are *Feedback, Caring and Assessment*, followed closely by *Scaffolding* and *Time on Task*. After that comes *Higher Order Thinking* and *Connections*. This makes sense to me given that I work with developmental learners. I am happy to see that *Caring* is another of the higher areas for me. . . . My early focus as an educator was in critical literary analysis. I believe that our students can

think and learn at a higher level and that challenging them to look deeper into text is a way of helping them become more proficient writers and deeper thinkers.

The authoritative set of pedagogy matters practice improvement model tags was derived from a qualitative analysis of the large volume of individual teaching behaviors captured digitally from the classroom practice documentation of the first faculty cohort of GSCC over an entire semester. The tags were later validated by triangulation and cross-referencing with student depictions of faculty behaviors and with the research literature (Yarnall et al., 2010; see the appendix for a full description of the development and definitions of the tags.) Our research demonstrates not only the validity of the tags but also that faculty members are able to apply the tags accurately to their own work with a high level of interrater reliability.

Twenty individual pedagogical tags are grouped into five themes. Each theme is distinguished by color, and each of the tags in a theme is represented by a shade of that color. This creates a strong visual representation of practice that develops fully over the weeks of teaching and documenting by each instructor (see Figure 3.5). The overarching pedagogical themes are

Figure 3.5   Themes and Tags

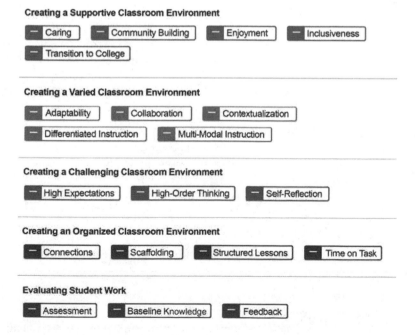

- creating a *supportive* classroom environment,
- creating a *varied* classroom environment,
- creating a *challenging* classroom environment,
- creating an *organized* classroom environment, and
- *evaluating* student work.

Teresa DiMonico, of Sinclair Community College in Ohio, said, "When I started to tag and comment on my colleagues' activities, I saw how valuable it is to focus and concentrate."

Kristin Duckworth, a math professor at Community College of Baltimore County in Maryland, said,

> This might be kind of a strange idea, but I wonder if we could "tag" ourselves as teachers, not just parts of our lessons. I think it would be interesting to see which three tags each of us would select to describe our overall teaching philosophy/style. If we did this maybe the assumption could then be that these themes were almost always going to be present in the background, but we would then highlight three others for each lesson that were perhaps more unique to that particular class session.

As we demonstrate later, highlighting and tagging Classroom Practice descriptions is important to the individual faculty member as an analytic frame for reflecting on the relationship between the teaching and the learning with a specific group of students. However, because highlights and tags were developed by practitioners and validated independently, they also provide an authoritative pedagogical language where none existed before, thereby giving faculty a means to engage one another in deep and detailed discussion. Katrina Nichols, a math professor at Delta Community College in Michigan, asserted, "I learned through the project how important it is to be mindful of multiple levels of execution when I teach (engagement, fun, technology, scaffolding, etc.). Knowing I had to tag lessons forced me to plan more thoroughly each day to involve more tags than I probably would have prior to the project."

Routine: Peer Practice Dialogue

The first major routine of the pedagogy matters model that we describe here is documenting the lesson, which involves recording the weekly lesson details and reflecting on them. The second routine involves highlighting and tagging the lesson. As we have noted, we have found this repeated reflective process that is based on adult learning theory to be meaningful to faculty, particularly because the work of highlighting and tagging lessons gives them the opportunity to think deeply about their teaching and its impact on their students. In the pedagogy matters practice improvement model the first two routines form the foundation for the third major routine: Peer Practice Dialogue. Here what we address is the independence, if not isolation, of the college professor as teacher and the power of peer insight to stimulate creativity and support problem solving.

Each week when a faculty member posts a Classroom Practice description, two faculty in the same discipline are assigned to read it and all the related posted artifacts. They are asked to comment and discuss it in a designated area connected to the lesson post on Classroom Notebook. The posting professor is asked to respond to the comments and questions from his or her colleagues. This dialogue among peers is a granular look at teaching practice and stimulates reflection and action by the reviewers and those reviewed. This *virtuous circle* is a distinctive attribute of the model and a key to sustained faculty engagement.

Let's return to Joyce Lindstrom and her flipped classroom.

After posting her Classroom Practice description, Joyce engages in Peer Practice Dialogue with several fellow math professors. Trisha White of Ozarks Technical College in Missouri offers a simple supportive statement: "Joyce, I think what you have done is awesome. You were willing to throw everything out the window and try something completely different. Amazing." Stephanie Fernandes, from Lewis and Clark Community College in Illinois, and Joan Smith, from Calhoun Community College in Alabama, ask Joyce the following questions: "Did all your students do the necessary at home work? Are there consequences for those who do not?" and "Do you use the textbook material/videos or do you find others online like Kahn Academy and YouTube or do you create your own? Do you provide any structured notes for them to complete while watching the video or do they just take notes as they feel beneficial?"

These questions from peers position Joyce as the expert on her own classroom and suggest that Joan and Stephanie might be interested in attempting this approach themselves. But the dialogue serves primarily to direct Joyce back to her own teaching and intentions, reflecting again on why to use a certain teaching strategy and amplifying her ability to improve her teaching.

When Joyce adds to the conversation by saying she is worried about how students perceive the assessments she asks them to complete, Stephanie responds, "Have you considered including more concept-oriented questions on the assessments to 'force' them to learn the concepts instead of just copying the method—since you indicate you are worried about that? Possibly include more writing/explanation questions?" Classroom Notebooks gives faculty a location to explore and play with their teaching ideas while receiving support and encouragement from colleagues who work with similar content and face similar teaching contexts.

In addition to the critical and valuable general exchange Joyce and her peers engaged in, the pedagogy matters practice improvement model encourages the commenting faculty to address their Peer Practice Dialogue, in significant part, to the choice of tags and the evidence provided in the lesson description for the tag selection. Tagging provides faculty with the focus and language for dialogue. We find that although faculty culture eschews criticism of pedagogical techniques and manifests extreme deference to peer teaching practices, the common lens of tagging provides a consistent set of parameters for talking about the teaching strategies used by peers. By focusing on the evidence for the selection of tags, faculty members are able to provide a supportive context for commenting on and expanding on one another's reflections. At the same time the typed conversation tends to cause poster and reader to push one another to greater rigor and authenticity in enacting strategies that really embody the tags they believe they are using. In this non-evaluative setting, peer input can be the most understanding and insightful feedback available to a college teacher. In the community setting this routine deepens interactions among faculty, thereby strengthening the commitment of individuals to the work of the whole.

Box G provides an abbreviated example of Peer Practice Dialogue, showing how peer comment combines close attention and professional support. In the lesson narrative by Elizabeth Nicoli-Suco, a math professor at Miami-Dade College in Florida, she describes using a wide variety of methods to try to help students understand several concepts—graphical representation of the slope-intercept form to write an equation of a line, graphing a linear equation, and so forth. The collegial support that emerges naturally ("another great lesson!") is part of the power of Peer Practice Dialogue because getting

---

Box G Peer Dialogue Using the Language of Tags (1)

Hi Elizabeth!

Thank you again for sharing your work—another great lesson! I loved your quiz after your lesson and think it is great to help students process all the material you covered that day. I find it generally has great benefits (i.e., the questions they ask each other and the "digging" in to understand and explain to each other). Do you see the same thing? . . . Per the tags: I agree with *Structure in Presentation*—you had a very structured step-by-step approach, with supporting mini lecture, while also being flexible to adapt to student needs. I thought the *Feedback* tag was appropriate and seen not only with the group quiz, but also as you were circulating the room during class answering every question students asked.

Other tags I thought of and am curious what you would think were: *Adaptability* and *Peer Engagement*[8] (which seems to me is a central part of your class structure? Is that true?) I am asking these questions as I thought it was central to my teaching but I have not tagged it once!

I thought of *Adaptability* in how you decided when to move on according to student reaction/ability/feedback. *Peer Engagement* was evident to me in your group quiz as well as your having students work together on problems during the "lecture" part of the class.

Sorry for writing so much! I get really excited as I read over all your work and your students' work. Thanks again!

Katrina Nichols, Delta Community College, Michigan

direct positive feedback on a specific lesson is a joy almost wholly unknown among college faculty. But discussing tag choices gives substance and texture to the conversation.

Tagging also grounds discussion as faculty struggle with a lack of success in moving students forward. Box H shows how Misty Evans, a developmental English professor from Murray State College in Kentucky, commiserates with Laurie McCartan, a developmental English professor from Metropolitan State University in Minnesota, over a video of a class that Laurie has posted. Despite the challenges of producing a video, it has high utility when included in the class narrative and incorporated into the overall reflection, tagged, and then used as the basis for Peer Practice Dialogue. In the video, we see Laurie teaching a lesson about the writing cycle and how students can identify a topic. She leads students in a discussion of the cultural norms that exist in any conversation, and she uses an example of the Hmong culture as a touch point. We see her providing her students with a handout intended to help them in selecting a topic, which she posts as part of her lesson description in Classroom Notebook. We see her working at the board outlining how to investigate cultural norms through writing.

Box H Peer Dialogue Using the Language of Tags (2)

Laurie,

I understand your frustration with *Higher Order Thinking*. Most days, my students have insightful comments and good writing to express them. Occasionally, I feel exasperated, and as therapy, I read a line or two from a student's formal writing assignment to a fellow teacher. We giggle at the vague language, awkward misspelling, or narrow view, and we contemplate the best way to help the writer.

To set the stage, I teach in Kentucky where most students are discouraged from traveling abroad by family, friends, and the media. I assigned a culture essay in one of my courses this semester and a student wrote about Mexico. His central point in one of his paragraph's [*sic*] illustrating Mexican culture: "The U.S. has given Mexicans an opportunity to a better life. If we didn't have Mexicans here, then we wouldn't be able to eat at Mexican restaurants." I wasn't sure how to respond to that for a bit. I ended up writing something like "What is it we find most appealing about their food and can you use that to express how their food reflects their culture?" On days like that, I convince myself that his exposure to other cultures on campus would surely broaden his perspective. Not something I would tag *Higher Order Thinking*. Unfortunately, he became frustrated with my comments and decided to skip revision.

I question my *Higher Order Thinking* tags often. At our institution, the freshman comp course requirement is English 105, only 1 entry level comp course. It's 4 credit hours covering Critical Reading, Writing, and Academic Inquiry. They teach classic lit, philosophy, literature, and research-based writing. I often question whether I am effectively preparing my students for the *Higher Order Thinking* necessary for success in English 105.

Misty Evans, Murray State College, Kentucky

McCartan tags her video *Higher Order Thinking* and *Transition to College* because she identified these areas as ones in which she wished to improve her teaching. Her peers, however, see the teaching in the video as containing broader themes. Box I contains snippets of the dialogue about the video. The exchange serves to highlight other issues that come into play in practice, all of which might affect the success of a specific teaching technique. The tenor of this conversation is collaborative ("I'm so going to use your 'work the circle'

Box I Peer Comments on Tags in Videos

I'm so going to use your "work the circle" activity, Laurie *and* I'm also looking up whether crocodiles do in fact have intestines. I concur with Misty and Mike's excellent commentary about the lesson and the video. You are adept at eliciting important insights from your students—the notions of "cultural commentary" and "trending topics" came from them and you were able to weave these perspectives into the overall conversation about the writing cycle. I agree that engaging them in this way is bringing them to *Higher Order Thinking* skills because it holds up ideas to multiple interpretations (analysis) and invites the students to choose the most relevant points (evaluation). You raise an interesting point about *Scaffolding* class participation. Often students do need an overt intervention here—a first thoughts, free write about a topic before you discuss it or have a chance to talk about it in a group, or a cocktail party in class to prime their thinking before discussion. Check out Pathfinder [the pedagogy matter's practice improvement online archive] using some of those for search terms and see if you find anything helpful.

Monica Stansberry, El Centro College, Texas

That's a great personal example about the Hmong culture. I didn't know what that was until your post intrigued me enough to look it up. It's always great when students open up and contribute in the discussion in a meaningful way with real-life experiences. I love the "Cycle of Composition" artifact you attached. It's a great method and I use something similar. I make the same circle on the board with arrows, but . . . the circle begins with "Brainstorm," and continues around to "Organize," "Write," "Revise," and ends with "Error Analysis." Regarding your Overall Reflection on your tags, I too was too concerned with 'comfort' and 'enjoyment' in the beginning of my teaching career. Now I still incorporate that in my lesson, but I focus more on the 'tough love' approach. I don't want to be too strict, but I don't want to be too lenient. I still make it comfortable, but I push them because their first language is not English.

Mike Sfiropoulos, Palm Beach State College, Florida

For example, you called out a student for "checking out about 3 minutes ago." You brought her back into the conversation. You also had a student who was distracted by the clock. You entertained his distraction for a bit by joking that your husband didn't see the point of the projection clock, but then quickly brought the students back to the topic. I think you should have also tagged *Presence.*[9] I also believe that you foster a fun classroom environment. Several times you made jokes, and I would tag *Enjoyment.* I would love to comment on the lesson's effectiveness, but I feel uncomfortable doing that without any student samples illustrating the completion of the Cycle of Composition handout. It was great watching your video.

Misty Evans, Murray State University, Kentucky

activity"), supportive ("You are adept at eliciting important insights from your students"; "I too was too concerned with 'comfort' and 'enjoyment' in the beginning of my teaching career"), but also challenging. One peer gently talks about how it is not possible to really know the effectiveness of the work because no formative assessments are posted ("I would love to comment on the lesson's effectiveness, but I feel uncomfortable doing that without any student samples illustrating the completion of the Cycle of Composition handout.").

Patterns

College teaching is a professional practice that is executed through multiple interactions over time with diverse groups of students. College teaching outcomes are presumed to be achieved incrementally as students learn to master the material, modes of inquiry, and habits of mind. Professional development activities are hard to tie to this moving river of interactions. If instructors want to change their teaching for the better, where do they start? This is not an idle question because, as we note in the introduction, if each faculty member teaching in the more than 125,000 developmental English and math classes each semester were able to help just four more students succeed, the effect would be a 14% increase in pass rates. This suggests that a nontrivial impact from small changes is achievable if faculty members can expand their teaching effectiveness for the range of students in their classes.

If we have come to know anything through our work, it is that it is hard to know what to change and even harder to introduce the change into practice effectively. We have found that repeated documenting, reflecting, tagging, and talking with peers about practice does provide the insight necessary for personal innovation in practice. Harnessing data to reveal an individual faculty member's pedagogical pattern can be the stimulus and proof point for action.

Throughout the course of a semester, a visual picture of what faculty do, self-reported via tags, emerges as a pattern that is generated automatically by Classroom Notebook (see Figure 3.6). The pattern enables faculty members to stand back from the specifics of lesson content and think more holistically about their teaching practice. They are repeatedly reminded in their work in the pedagogy matters practice improvement community that their objective is to help more students learn more deeply. This motivation, combined with the evidence of their practice that the pattern reflects, helps faculty members take the initiative to experiment in an intentional way with one or more elements of their well-worn practice and to assess and discuss the impact of the change with their peers. The simple but potent power of an image to prompt change is remarkable.

Each instructor's unique pattern for a semester appears to be stable before the sixth week of class, and a preliminary examination suggests that patterns may be stable significantly earlier in the semester. The visual image, an actual picture of what a professor *looks like* in class, serves several purposes.

Figure 3.6   A Faculty Member's Cumulative Semester Pedagogical Pattern Through Self-Tagging

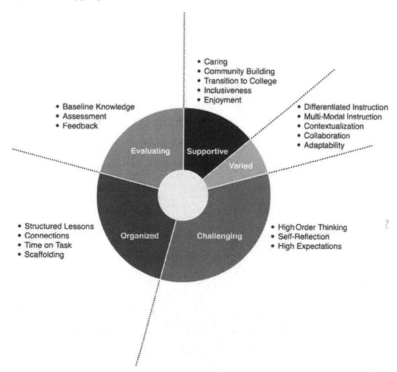

The first purpose is that this personal picture is a reality check for the faculty member. In the rush of teaching, faculty may believe they are pushing for *Higher Order Thinking*, but their reflections and tags shown in their pattern from Classroom Notebook may not corroborate this perception. The mirror of a pattern, therefore, enhances honest self-reflection because the granularity and specificity of the classroom narrative and reflection, accompanied by examples of student work and depicted by a pattern of tags, combine to create input that fascinates and provokes.

The second, and arguably the most important, purpose of the pedagogical pattern is to give the faculty member a guide to innovation, adoption, or adaptation of new teaching practices, customized for the class he or she is teaching at the moment. Recognizing that there is no perfect pattern, no individual template all faculty can aspire to, each professor can look at his or her pattern and determine which elements to balance through the next weeks. For example, a faculty member whose pattern shows tagging a lot of *Creating a Challenging Classroom Environment* might see a small number of tags in the *Supportive Classroom* theme and, therefore, take steps to incorporate *Community Building* approaches in future classes. By having a relatively accurate (though admittedly self-reported) pattern, each faculty member can pinpoint where he or she might change to be more effective with the students in the class in a given semester. Mike Sfiropoulos, an English professor at Palm Beach State College in Florida, notes:

> The patterns have helped me to "see" my teaching come to life. They are helpful because I can see where I am focusing most of my time when I prepare lessons, so in turn it gives me the opportunity to redirect my efforts to include important themes that I may not be incorporating into my lessons.

The third purpose of the teaching pattern is the role it plays in promoting honest dialogue among faculty peers. In a post to her peer reviewers, Bronte Miller of Patrick Henry Community College in Virginia, bemoans how hard it is to change, "I have every intention of trying some of the new strategies I think might help my students, but I go into class and plunge ahead the way I've always taught. Changing my own teaching is harder than I thought." The clarity of a visual pattern based on specific tags forms the basis of communication among participants and makes honest reflection unavoidable. The Peer Practice Dialogue routine, in which faculty members discuss one another's lessons, tags, and patterns, yields insights and helps move intentions to actions. The pattern not only provides guidance to an individual faculty member about how to improve, but also, by watching and commenting on the changes (or lack thereof) with peers over time, reinforces the difficulty and the joy of real change expressed in practice.

As faculty review their pedagogical patterns, they have a clear depiction of the actions they take to teach their students. Because they aspire to be successful with more students, they want to change, expand, or deepen what they do. While understanding what needs to be done to achieve the goal of improving as a professional is easy, implementing the actions necessary to achieve that goal can be hard. Peer support is essential to changing ingrained pedagogical patterns. The isolation of faculty practice can be enervating, and having a peer see one's work, really understand it in all its dimensions, and appreciate when it is being done well, is a boon. This is particularly true for adjunct faculty who are too often thrown into teaching a course with the bare minimum of teaching support structures. The insight and support of a professional peer community can make a significant difference in effectiveness.

Figure 3.7 provides an example of a highlighted and tagged reflection by Larry Giddings, an English professor at Pikes Peak Community College in Colorado. In this post he explains how the tagged actions were attempts to alter his teaching pattern in ways he thought would benefit the students he was teaching that semester.

He chose four instances of his work to highlight, encompassing four different tags and three thematic areas that his analysis of his pattern led him to specify as areas to alter his approach. Close observation of his changing pattern is a feedback mechanism to determine whether he was successful in changing his practice in the way he wished. The dialogue with peers about these elements can further reinforce and refine his actions.

Figure 3.7   Highlighting and Assigning Tags

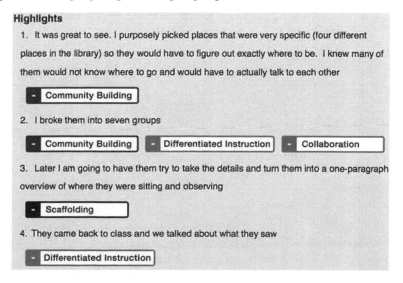

Patterns Writ Large

When we examine the patterns of all faculty members participating in pedagogy matters, we see some interesting preliminary findings. The first is that a faculty member's use of specific strategies, as revealed by their self-tagged pattern, does not appear to change as a semester progresses (Yarnall et al., 2010). That is, there appear to be no dramatic differences in the way professors teach early in the semester compared to their teaching in the middle or toward the end. The second preliminary finding is that an instructor's pattern does change semester to semester (Yarnall, Feng, Dornsife, Werner, Fusco, Tidwell-Morgan, Ngo, & Gallagher, 2011). As a consequence of conversations with faculty participants, we tentatively conclude that this is a result of faculty customizing their teaching practices to the specific kinds of students in a particular class. Experienced faculty, in particular, have a repertoire of activities and modes of teaching, a personal storehouse of ways to help students learn. When faced with an engaged and motivated class, faculty might offer ways for students to accelerate through differently challenging problems. Conversely, faculty might face a class of students who possess poor academic skills or problematic behavioral issues, often resulting in a hostile classroom climate. For the latter kind of class, faculty might focus initially on building community or carefully stepping students through scaffolding so that early success begets better engagement. As Laurillard (2008b) reminds us, classroom interactions are an ongoing dynamic of give and take, and the specific circumstances of student plus teacher plus topic plus environment calls for differentiated responses. We think, therefore, that pedagogical patterns are distinctively connected to a specific class, and that focused change happens slowly with experimentation over a semester.

We also do not find that some patterns are better or worse. No specific pattern is more closely associated with student success than others, although this finding may change upon examination of a much larger amount of faculty and student data. The art of teaching is revealed in the patterns, and many different patterns work well for individual instructors. The teaching patterns are flexible, personal, and full of heuristics, giving an overview of what has occurred to date in a classroom and then serving as a guide for recalibrating future teaching interactions. The extraordinary individuality of teachers, as expressed in their patterns, is the generator of the energy in a classroom.

Notes

1. In the development process of the model, we have sought to identify the minimum number of activities or routines required to produce the insights necessary for the work. This remains a work in progress.
2. All faculty quotes throughout the text are from the pedagogy matters project's online platform and are used with permission.
3. A flipped classroom refers to the way a professor presents content. In general, the lecture material is posted by the professor online. Students are required to do readings and watch the lecture as homework, and in-class time is used for individual, group, and full class discussion and problem solving.
4. Joyce is referring to a practice she adapted from Bronte Miller, a colleague in her group.
5. This refers to Stephanie's focus on changing aspects of her teaching practices that she has set as her professional development goals, based on her analysis of her pattern (patterns are described later in this chapter).
6. We see enormous change, however, in the technical feasibility of video recording, which makes spur-of-the-moment or planned recordings eminently doable.
7. All images presented in this book are in black and white. However, in Classroom Notebook all tags are color coded by theme. See book images in color at https://takingcollege teachingseriously.kpublic.net/home
8. Peer Engagement, which was a tag in the first cohort of GSCC, has been renamed Collaboration to reflect the current evolution of tags
9. Presence, which was the original tag, is now renamed Inclusiveness.

4

Scaffolding the Community 1

Coaching and Sharing

Teaching college students is not only difficult but also extremely isolating. The literature reinforces the hunger for dialogue about teaching among many college faculty members (Bass, 2012a, 2012b; Huber & Hutchings, 2005; Hutchings & Schulman, 1999). Drawing on the literature and experience of communities of practice, the pedagogy matters practice improvement model incorporates structured social interaction and collaborative group work because these are crucial factors in practice improvement (Lave & Wenger, 1991). Individual and group work are interlocking and interdependent elements that foster and support experimentation and change by faculty. Neither element alone ensures the result and a vibrant and productive community of independent professionals requires a particular type of guidance. The pedagogy matters practice improvement model strives to balance a design born of research and experience with a flexibility that responds to the context and characteristics of each faculty cohort. The key people to walk this line are the peer coaches.

Appreciative Coaching

Given the lack of experience with, and indeed the sensitivity of faculty members toward, a focus on pedagogical practice improvement, the pedagogy matters practice improvement model operates independently of institutional evaluation processes. Instead, it is designed to promote iterative improvement by building an engaged community of mutually supportive peers that depends and capitalizes on the establishment of respect and trust. This does not, however, mean that peer relationships are passively endorsing. Rather, we seek to establish an intense experience of personal and group growth. To achieve this we design structured interactions, provide the language of tags to frame dialogue, and relentlessly incorporate evidence of student learning so that the trajectory linking experimentation and improvement is as clear and straightforward as possible. To support faculty in maximally using the elements of the model quickly and well, we rely on a team of peer coaches who are able to establish, model, and maintain high engagement and assist faculty in stretching their performance by nurturing a community where expectations are high and taking risks is encouraged and supported. As noted in our theory of change, discussed in Chapter 2, personal improvement practices are best achieved in this context.

In the pedagogy matters practice improvement model, a group of faculty members is divided into small discipline-based *pedagogy circles* of six or seven people. The pedagogy circle is the context for the dominant routines of the pedagogy matters experience because the members of the pedagogy circle are one another's interlocutors. Each circle has a peer coach who acts as the organizer, task master, inspiration and cheerleader for the group.

Peer coaches are graduates of a pedagogy matters practice improvement experience. This means that they not only are active teaching faculty engaged in the same kind of work as the circle members but also have internalized the pedagogy matters practice improvement model and are well positioned to guide others. Coaches are selected because they are articulate, respectful, and responsive. They have a positive attitude toward teaching and learning and, ideally, bring that all-important quality of a sense of humor to their work. A good coach is able to quickly gauge and respond to the needs of his or her circle and help each faculty member in the circle fully use the tools and routines.

Coaches post weekly, reminding the faculty in their circle about upcoming routines, due dates, and other administrative information. However, two contributions stand out. First, coaches read all posts made by all faculty members in the circle weekly. They provide faculty with feedback on their Classroom Practice descriptions and offer questions and thoughts to prompt deeper reflection and discussion among peers. This dialogue is visible to all members of the circle. In this way the coaches model, in a substantive fashion, the kind of feedback that supports growth. Second, the coaches identify topics and structure collaborative group work that allows

Figure 4.1   Appreciative Coaching

Wow, am I impressed. I would (if I could) tag your responses:

- Higher Order Thinking
- Community Building
- Mastery and
- Appreciative Inquiry (a tag I just made up)

In other words, you all did wonderfully detailed, thoughtful, and appreciative responses to your fellow team members. In addition you created multiple levels of conversation by citing each other's posts and responding to each other in the Comments section. I was very impressed with the expertise and critical thinking in evidence there.

About Appreciative Inquiry

In fact, I was going to append here a "primer for appreciative inquiry that you might read in your spare time ⊠ but your actual postings alert me to the fact that you are already showing mastery of delving more deeply into the nuances of tags and the outcome-evidence connections in each other's work. Truly-Good Game!

Note: I'll still attach the primer here just in case. One disclaimer-it includes lots of questions. Do not feel that you need to use more than two or so in responding to each other and DO feel free to adapt the questions to your own style and voice.

About Photos on the CN Faculty Page:
If you have not had a chance to post a picture yet in CN, please try to. Not sure if you did??----if you can't see your photo when you look at the Faculty page then you didn't. Having a picture up reminds us that we are those individuals the community we met in NYC!

About Sunday Night Comment Circle:
I didn't foreground this enough last week BUT on Sunday nights we'd like the people who were scheduled to post to "circle" back to the responses you received and answer any questions from your colleagues or provide specific examples requested. In this way, we can close the feedback loop and make sure everyone feels "heard"

About Trends:
In our Coaches/Team conference call last Friday, Marisa showed us the "word cloud" created by the tags in Week 1. I was fascinated by the predominance of words such as "community building," "assessment," "comfort," and "structure in presentation." Wouldn't you agree that these are indeed the elements of a lesson we foreground in the first week! The word cloud indicates that Math faculty and English faculty alike are focusing on the activities students need to be successful in these first weeks. Very cool, (Wordle/Work Cloud is fun to use as a brainstorming model since patterns emerge and these help students organize their thinking. I included the link above)

About This Week: September 3

Posts	Responds
Misty	Larry and Mike respond to Misty
Larry	Laura and Judi respond to Larry
Judi	Larry and Mike respond to Judi
Mike	Misty and Monica respond to Mike
Laura	Monica and Judi respond to Laura

About Conversations and Community:

Friday night I saw David Hwang's play Chinglish at Berkeley Rep. It's about an Ohioan who travels to a small city in China to create a market for correctly translated signs for the new cultural center. More than that, it's about language and translation and how difficult it is to connect with words over cultural distances. In many ways, as we work together, not only here in GSCC but also in our own departments, we recognize the how pedagogical practice and theory sometimes "lost in translation" from one classroom to another. Our work here helps us create and maintain a teaching community where we are speaking the same language, one that leads to success for our students and support for our own work. Very cool indeed.

Have a great September week! Business as usual this week and then next week we have our first Monthly Fellows Seminar. More later!

Don't forget to write/question/nudge/kvetch/share   success!

Show parent I Reply

the full circle membership to work together to address common issues arising from individual practice reflections. We have found that by grouping faculty by discipline with a coach of the same content background and by requiring faculty to engage in a specified set of activities, individually and collectively, we create a level of intimacy that deepens individual reflection and establishes the trust necessary for thoughtful group engagement. Figure 4.1 is an example of English professor Rosemary Arca's *Scoop*, a weekly newsletter she uses to inform faculty in her circle of the expectations of them for the week.

Coaches' Community of Practice

In the pedagogy matters practice improvement model, we expect, and indeed want, to create a dynamic experience because no two pedagogy circles are ever the same. The model is designed to be adaptive in real time, requiring the coaches to monitor, share, and debate the experiences of participating faculty and adjust and adapt to them. We ensure this feedback loop by having the coaches collaborate in their own structured community of practice that we call the *coaches' circle*. They record and reflect on their work in online posts, discuss the impact of their coaching with one another, and develop action steps that they implement individually or together. The structured coaching process is codified in a coaching curriculum and can be accessed at https://takingcollege teachingseriously.kpublic.net/about.

The coaches also maintain an active online *coaches' corner*, a designated private space for coaches in Classroom Notebook. Interactions in the corner are unstructured; this is a place for postings about anything that arises in coaching work—a quick question, a request for help or affirmation, or a way to share resources. In the following comment posted by coach Rosemary Arca in the coaches' corner, she is calling out the challenge of the role, looking for affirmation, if not empathy, from her fellow coaches.

> I then thought long and hard about attitude, meaning the coaching attitude. Because I've taught online classes forever, I know how important it is to establish a persona, one that creates a human connection in a virtual world. Being an English geek I also know the power of language so I intentionally used inclusive language and "we/our/us" as a way to create a community. I pretty much typed to my circle as I talked. Another aspect of attitude is the ability to effectively praise, nudge, challenge, and call out while maintaining an effective coaching relationship. This is always hard for me to calibrate. In a coaching of peers situation it's quite a complex dance because we're equals.

Cross-Disciplinary Engagement

Fully two thirds of the time invested by individual faculty in the pedagogy matters practice improvement experience is spent on the weekly Classroom Practice descriptions, Highlighting and Tagging, and Peer Practice Dialogue. Almost all the remaining third of the time goes to group activities, not only within pedagogy circles but also across a larger cross-disciplinary group to further stimulate faculty thinking and deepen a commitment to honing practice. We find that structured and moderated cross-disciplinary groupings are valuable because they help a faculty member who is a content expert in one area to see pedagogy in practice in a different content area. Yasser Hassebo, a mathematics professor at LaGuardia Community College in New York, commented in a post that working with the English faculty helped him understand that knowing definitions of words was a deeper issue than he had previously considered when asking his students to complete applied math problems. The issues and ideas that arise pedagogically across disciplines enrich the options and understandings for all. Several different kinds of online group activities are worthwhile, and each serves a purpose, for example, giving prominence to effective practices or providing just-in-time conversations about emergent issues. All strengthen the personal and professional bonds among faculty.

Routine: The Practice Showcase: "One of My Best . . ."

In the semester-long multidisciplinary Practice Showcase, faculty present "one of their best" teaching strategies, approaches, or activities—anything that they find to be especially effective. One or two faculty will make a presentation in any month. In this public way, faculty shine a light on something in their practice they feel is innovative and important. Similar in format to a conference presentation, this presentation is audio- or videotaped and posted in the community so that everyone can view the presentation on their own time and comment asynchronously about the practice and the issues it raises.

For an idea of the quality of interaction, let's look at the exchange in Figure 4.2 between Kate Smith, a mathematics faculty member at Monroe Community College in western New York, and Elizabeth Clark, an English professor at LaGuardia Community College in New York City. Kate Smith posted a presentation in the Practice Showcase in which she describes how she has current students interview former developmental mathematics students who have gone on to be successful in their college classes and in their later careers. She speaks about the value these interviews seem to have for her current and former students. Elizabeth Clark's comments indicate not only that she is inspired by Smith's project, but also that it causes her to reflect

Figure 4.2   Sharing Teaching Practices in Dialogue With Peers

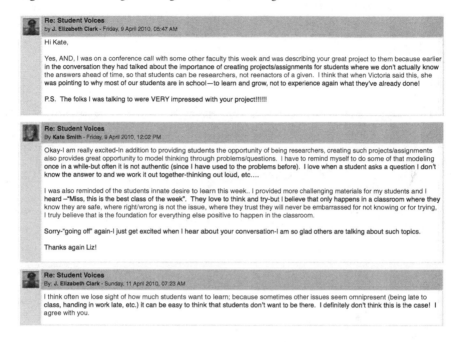

on the value of this type of assignment in building specific student skills. This is characteristic of Practice Showcase exchanges—faculty interrogate one another's strategies and identify their own learning from observing an activity or project. These experiences serve to help the presenter refine his or her thinking and build the bonds of substantive ideas across a diverse group of faculty.

We find that interaction in a group activity functions most effectively when the ethos is one of thoughtful sharing, where differences are acknowledged but not seen as the impetus to convince one another of the primacy of one's approach. The presentations can be at any level of granularity—a semester, a subject, a lesson, or even part of a lesson—and on any aspect of pedagogy from design to content to assessment. The goal is for faculty to present their best, most exciting, and most innovative work. A set of questions guides the presentation (e.g., What did you do? Can you describe what happened in the classroom? What was the impact on students? How do you know?).

Faculty acknowledge that while a presentation involves some work, they appreciate being able to look carefully at one another's practices (Yarnall, Feng, Dornsife, Werner, et al., 2011). Examples of presentation topics presented by faculty include "Using Blackboard in My Introductory Algebra

---

Box J   Practice Showcase: "Students Use of Notebooks in Basic Math"

I do not collect and grade all homework because of the time element. For the same reason, I have not done formal notes, although I definitely do see the advantages. Have either of you experimented with My Math Lab or similar products?

Eric Kraus, Sinclair Community College, Ohio

Thank you for your really useful presentation. A couple of times in the past, I had tried requiring students to keep a notebook but the grading of it was fairly subjective (and therefore I didn't make it worth much). I found your rubric/scoring sheet very inspiring and I'm going to try again, this time making the points much more concrete.

Yasser Hassebo, LaGuardia Community College, New York

Class," "Cooperative English," "Teaching Students to Write a Critique," "Addressing Affective Factors Through Student Writing," and "ePortfolio and the Basic Writing Classroom."

The following excerpt is from a presentation by Katrina Nichols of Delta Community College in Michigan, titled "Student Use of Class Notebooks in Basic Math." Katrina used free Jing software to demonstrate her notebook requirements and rubrics to her peers in Classroom Notebook.[1] Comments from peers on Katrina's Jing are in Box J. As an organizer, planner, and study guide, the notebook effective learning systematically facilitates. It helps to build student performance confidence and addresses different learning styles and needs. In the classroom, students are guided to utilize time management skills, to self-assess their progress regularly, to practice assessment techniques, and to make connections.

Routine: Community Jam

Another large group activity is a Jam, a structured and moderated asynchronous exchange. Often a Jam is scheduled in response to an issue the coaches have found to be of widespread interest or concern. For example, many faculty members are unfamiliar with and somewhat resistant to formative assessment, so a community-wide Jam on this topic, moderated by the coaches, presents an opportunity for everyone to ask their questions and talk about ideas.

A Jam takes place over one or more days in order to allow faculty members to read and respond as their time permits. The structure might be a single thread or multiple threads addressing different aspects of the overall topic. As in all work in Classroom Notebook, participants who post during the Jam are always identified by name and photograph.

The following is a post by Robin Ozz, a developmental English professor at Phoenix College in Arizona, from a Jam about the relationship between formative and summative assessment.

> I had the same thoughts about which was most important, the immediate feedback on a small lesson or the retention of the ideas to do well on an exam or quiz. Some students need time to "digest" the concepts and for these students, the assessment right after the lesson is never good. Others can do well at the end of class, but forget the material by the next class period or maybe on the exam. I've been doing both types of assessment this quarter (formative and summative), and I am seeing a connection between the students that get the ideas by the end of the lesson and those that get it overall. No real surprise here, but I think the number of students who "need time to digest" is smaller than I thought.

Next is a post by Peter Adams, a developmental English professor at Community College of Baltimore County in Maryland, on the value of formative assessment.

> Thanks for the thoughtful explanation of formative assessment. You've clarified the evidence gathering activity for me considerably. In fact, this entire Jam has led me to examine how I know what works and what doesn't much more deeply than I ever have before. And I am sure I will be continuing that examination throughout the two years we're spending together and after.

Sharing Resources

An interesting and valuable by-product of active pedagogy matters practice improvement communities is capturing specific practice descriptions in the context of the lessons in which they were taught. People are often tempted to create repositories of documents and large libraries of materials, but we recommend resisting doing this. Repositories are difficult to build, become outdated quickly, and, sadly, are too often neither actively nor consistently used.

The pedagogy matters practice improvement model includes an online tool called Pathfinder, a dynamic database that captures and organizes faculty member teaching practices using the taxonomy of tags augmented with keywords. It is intended as an up-to-date resource to spur faculty experimentation in the classroom by allowing faculty to review and then adopt or adapt what colleagues have used or simply as inspiration to create something new after seeing what is possible. Pathfinder is not just a list of curricular structures or activities; it opens the door to the teaching in practice. A search in Pathfinder brings the community participant to the Classroom Notebook narrative. This allows an instructor to see not only a new idea or approach to teaching but also how a peer implemented the practice, where it was used in the semester, and how students responded to the approach. In addition, the instructor can read the creator's reflection on what worked well or poorly in the class. Pathfinder, therefore, provides access to the richness of knowledge in context, elevating that knowledge beyond a narrow description to a richly detailed level that acknowledges the complexity of college teaching as practice.

In a mathematics Pedagogy Circle discussion about the use of contextualization, Cathy Montero from Northern Virginia Community College in Virginia found the work of two of her colleagues helpful.

> I looked at Pathfinder and found several good examples of contextualization. Arlene and Doug both posted problems involving a quadratic representing the path of a thrown ball or a bullet shot from a gun. I really liked Steve's example of the volume of a cylinder using M&M's. Those were just two of some really good examples.

Figure 4.3 provides a snippet of how searching in Pathfinder can be accomplished using multiple variables—discipline, faculty name, keyword, or pedagogical tag—individually or in combination. For example, a writing faculty member interested in improving the climate of student support in the classroom might find new affective activities by searching the tag "Inclusiveness" or by searching by the name of a peer whom he or she thinks is particularly good at creating an inclusive climate in the classroom. The instructor could also limit this search to examples of Inclusiveness used in the context of a particular lesson topic, such as revision, for example (see Figure 4.3).

The idea here is that sharing is a normal faculty practice. However, sharing usually happens within the immediate geographical area of a professor's life, typically with those who are physically nearest. Pathfinder expands this community by allowing faculty members to share their common lessons and ideas, even though they may never have met in person. It promotes a focus on a deeper understanding of the potential of new aspects of teaching methodologies such as scaffolding, learning, or creating metacognitive experiences for students that are grounded in practice and theory. And it shows teaching where the lesson occurs and then allows further exploration of resources, student work, and a faculty member's reflection on why something did or did not succeed in the class.

Figure 4.3   Searching in Pathfinder

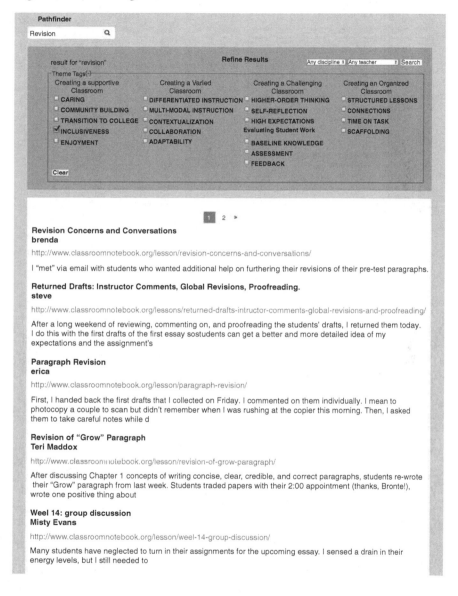

1 2 »

Revision Concerns and Conversations
brenda

http://www.classroomnotebook.org/lesson/revision-concerns-and-conversations/

I "met" via email with students who wanted additional help on furthering their revisions of their pre-test paragraphs.

Returned Drafts: Instructor Comments, Global Revisions, Proofreading.
steve

http://www.classroomnotebook.org/lessons/returned-drafts-intructor-comments-global-revisions-and-proofreading/

After a long weekend of reviewing, commenting on, and proofreading the students' drafts, I returned them today. I do this with the first drafts of the first essay sostudents can get a better and more detailed idea of my expectations and the assignment's

Paragraph Revision
erica

http://www.classroomnotebook.org/lesson/paragraph-revision/

First, I handed back the first drafts that I collected on Friday. I commented on them individually. I mean to photocopy a couple to scan but didn't remember when I was rushing at the copier this morning. Then, I asked them to take careful notes while d

Revision of "Grow" Paragraph
Teri Maddox

http://www.classroomnotebook.org/lesson/revision-of-grow-paragraph/

After discussing Chapter 1 concepts of writing concise, clear, credible, and correct paragraphs, students re-wrote their "Grow" paragraph from last week. Students traded papers with their 2:00 appointment (thanks, Bronte!), wrote one positive thing about

Weel 14: group discussion
Misty Evans

http://www.classroomnotebook.org/lesson/weel-14-group-discussion/

Many students have neglected to turn in their assignments for the upcoming essay. I sensed a drain in their energy levels, but I still needed to

Note

1. Another colleague, Reid Sunahara, of Kapi'olani Community College in Hawai'i, taught the large group how to use Jing because he found it a free and easy way to record a short video for his students. Its use rapidly spread among GSCC faculty.

5

Scaffolding the Community 2

Norms and Infrastructure

The pedagogy matters practice improvement model draws heavily from the literature on, and from examples of, successful online communities of practice. If there is a spectrum of effective community of practice designs, the pedagogy matters practice improvement model is at the most structured and focused end. This is because the goal of practice improvement is clear to all who participate and because the focus is explicitly on assessing change in faculty teaching *and* student learning. We rely on community of practice design principles for the administrative framework and for the culture of respectful and substantive dialogue so crucial to faculty practice improvement. Clear role definitions and supportive technological elements all serve to complement the routines that guide faculty in their work. In this chapter, we outline some of the structures that create a lively community space that is supportive and purposeful.

Personal Profiles

Faculty online communities that create trust and engender active participation cannot be anonymous. As in any social environment, the first rule of thumb is to introduce oneself. In the pedagogy matters practice improvement community, the user profile functions as an initial introduction to the community and an ongoing reference point. The profile makes individual faculty visible as professionals. The profiles also give insight into the personal side of each instructor by including photos of family or favorite activities, poems and quotes, or the things that make a faculty member a unique contributor to a college. In this way they support the social dimension of the community.

Figure 5.1   Example of a Faculty Profile

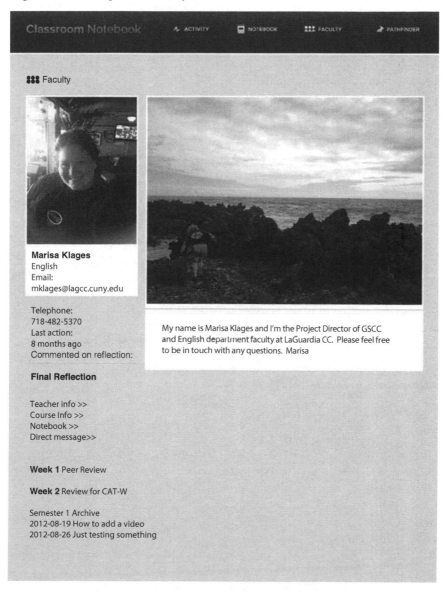

The basic elements of the profile are part of the Classroom Notebook platform; however, in an early community-building exercise, the group determines whether and how to expand the profile elements to suit its collective interests and desire for connection. We have found that photos of members serve an important function in building community and enabling people to "see" one another online (see Figure 5.1). When a photograph of the instructor accompanies all posts, the human being who is writing is always salient in the interaction.

The development of a vibrant sense of community must be authentic and not contrived because only in an authentic environment can a group of faculty members maintain their investment in the work over one or two semesters. We begin to build relationships and cultural norms immediately by convening a faculty group when we open the Classroom Notebook site and before the cycle of lesson posting begins. Group members are invited to register on the site, fill out their profile, post the all-critical picture, and introduce themselves in a nonstructured open space we call the coffee klatch.

The coaches complete all the registration and technical steps before the faculty members go online, which allows the cohort of faculty to meet the coaches and see and understand what is expected at this stage so they can emulate it. We then hold a first Jam for the full group, which requires no preparation on the faculty's part. The topic of the Jam is intended primarily to focus on their professional side in order to set the tone for the ensuing work, but at the same time to begin to reveal something personal about themselves so the relational side of community building can begin. We might ask, for example, Why do you teach? or What is your teaching philosophy?

Etiquette and Community Norms

The Power of Satisfaction

In a vibrant pedagogy matters practice improvement community, members see it as their responsibility to regularly check in, post their lesson narratives on a timely basis, read the comments of others, post their own comments, and participate actively in community activities. While these behavioral norms, like the norms of all groups, can be suggested and nurtured, it is impossible to mandate compliance. If faculty members are to put in the energy to participate and improve their practice, their core motivation—their point of passion—must necessarily draw from two sources. First, they must derive great satisfaction from reflecting in collaboration with peers on work in progress in the *moving present* of their classrooms. Second, they must be open to and value the guidance and support of peers as they experiment with improving their practice. Indeed, we do find that the energy of intrinsic satisfaction, supporting faculty in their quest to achieve student success, does foster healthy community norms over time. Satisfaction is not, of course, the same as fun, because the work of the community is serious and often hard. In guiding a pedagogy matters practice improvement community, therefore, careful attention has to be paid to how we make individuals visible as members of the community and how we cultivate the norms that support a generous and purposeful environment so that we scaffold faculty work and make the satisfaction they derive from engagement real and meaningful.

When and How Norms Are Set

Some of the norms of interaction in a community are set early as the community revs up and the practice improvement process is introduced. For example, norms about response time to one another's posts are established by each pedagogy circle at the start of its work and are evident when broken (faculty post apologies to one another for tardiness). Other norms of interaction are more emergent. For example, we find that the first Jams tend to be slightly formal and polite. Activities that break that formality (e.g., posting pictures of one's workspace) can be used to nudge the etiquette of a group in a more relaxed direction. The tone of early posts by coaches can also help the community find its voice. We emphasize the value of humor, or at least lightheartedness, in dialogue because it serves to build the bonds of connection.

To establish a reflective community, it is important to outline the routines of the work process clearly from the start and to orient each and every instructor to the platform so that he or she knows where to look in Classroom Notebook for information and to complete work. It is also important to explain why we have found the particular routines we have developed to be the most efficient way for each person to explore and deepen his or her own practice. Nonetheless, each faculty cohort is different, and we present the routines as the activity baseline; that is, the minimum level of action we have found to be effective. We consider this to be the *flexible core* that can and must be modified by and for each faculty cohort to suit its context. We encourage and support an open and lively dialogue that allows faculty members and coaches to continually assess whether the activities and time frames are working for the group. This flexibility to adapt within a clear framework is vital to maintaining the intensity of the community over time.

Clear deadlines for posting lessons in Classroom Notebook are a critical, albeit seemingly administrative, element of the pedagogy matters practice improvement model. This is because the important routines of the experience are only valuable to the individual in terms of personal growth if they recur consistently over time. Obviously, inconsistent posting also diminishes significantly the learning opportunity for peer reviewers. In a pedagogy matters practice improvement community the numerous recurring date-based routines include the Classroom Practice narrative and reflection, with its associated supporting documentation, examples of student work, and formative assessments; Highlighting and Tagging of the lesson; Peer Practice Dialogue comments; and a number of pedagogy circle and full-group online events. Members of a circle may mutually agree to alter a posting date, but a date itself is nonnegotiable because the time line gives faculty the clarity to be accountable to one another.

The balance struck between flexibility and rigidity must always lean in favor of practice—can faculty reasonably engage in the actions desired given the intensity of a semester, the demands of academic work, and the vagaries of life? Perhaps, not surprisingly, we have found that students are not the only group that can use a little brushing up on time management. Faculty often comment that they want to partake more fully in the activities of the community but find the specific demands of their jobs and lives are inhibitors. The following, posted in a Jam by Robin Ozz of Phoenix Community College in Arizona, is a suggestion about a way to change the pedagogy matters routines. She suggests reducing the requirement to explicitly experiment with practice to two times per semester. We held fast to the much more frequent and regular incidence as essential to improvements in the student experience but understood and appreciated where the request was coming from and used her suggestion as an opportunity to engage with the faculty about the underpinnings of the model:

> Continue with (practice description/reflection) and peer review. This has added immensely to my practice. Require at least two lessons per semester in which the faculty tries a completely innovative approach he/she has thought of or is an adaptation of what someone else had done, and report on the results. I am writing this with all the respect I have in my soul, as I do appreciate being a member of this wonderful venture that I am positive will take developmental education to another level.

While the coaches, the routines of the model, and the design of the Classroom Notebook platform all contribute in different ways to the behavior of participants, ultimately the hallmark of a vital community is its capacity to self-regulate because faculty must be the ultimate arbiter of the community's agreed-upon etiquette.

Open Space

Open space for unstructured dialogue is an important component of a sustained community. In the pedagogy matters practice improvement model, this space is the coffee klatch, which might be likened to a faculty lounge. It is an unstructured online space available 24 hours a day, seven days a week, for any and all topics. It is used for community announcements, logistics, and all manner of conversation, serious and frivolous. Faculty posts range from general queries about technology tools to questions about how to handle a classroom or campus issue. It contributes to a sense of community and builds trust among the faculty. Faculty participants celebrate births and awards, talk about everything from great movies to bad conferences, and share the best new YouTube video used in class. Not unlike Starbucks, it can be one of the most popular places on the Classroom Notebook platform. Additionally, because the coffee klatch is digital it can be analyzed to gain insight about the issues and opportunities that concern the group (see Box K).

Box K Conversation in Open Space

I see that you want us to innovate on a higher level, but I think this requires more time. . . . While I love our pedagogy circle discussions and look forward to this interaction with my colleagues, I'm not the best communicator in the written form and sometimes what I am trying to say or suggest is not articulated well in this format. . . . In fact for the first time I feel safe. I feel like my colleagues will tell me what they think and they will do it in a way that helps me grow. However, I . . . can't say the same thing for my math colleagues at [my college]. In fact, I spent most of my career hiding what I was doing because I knew that the senior faculty would not approve.

Mathematics professor whose name is withheld upon request

I am currently part of the Virginia Developmental English Redesign Team. We are redesigning everything about teaching dev. [developmental] reading and writing from the ground up, to make it more consistent throughout the system (placement, prerequisites, structure, etc.). Teachers who are *not* on the redesign team all express the same fear: that they are going to be told *how* to teach the material, and this isn't true at all. They are afraid of losing their autonomy. Is cherishing and protecting our autonomy necessarily a bad thing?

Michelle Zollars, Patrick Henry Community College, Virginia

The incredible resources and ideas my colleagues give me each week help me be a better teacher who has far more proverbial tools in her belt than ever before. Because of this project I am expecting and getting more from my students than ever. And this is all because of my participation in the project. My learning curve is steep, perhaps, but I am making progress because of the opportunities afforded me here. For that I, and my students, are grateful and better for it.

Peter Adams, Community College of Baltimore County, Maryland

The Community Manager

A successful community for reflective teaching practice improvement requires a community manager. In the abundant literature regarding online community management (Booth, 2011; Cambridge, Kaplan, & Suter, 2005; Fini, 2008; Owyang, 2008; Rosenbush, 2013), there is a general consensus about the roles the community manager must play. These role expectations hold true for the pedagogy matters practice improvement community; indeed, our experience suggests that the model will not work without a dedicated and experienced community manager.

The community manager is the chief of operations and administration in the community. The position's authority comes from a deep familiarity with faculty culture and experience with every facet of the work that coaches and faculty encounter in working with the pedagogy matters model in Classroom Notebook. The community manager builds relationships within the community, creates value for members who participate in the community, and acts as point person for issues of fidelity to the model. Among the many essential functions that might be assigned to a community manager, the most important are

- serving as the helpdesk, dealing with technical issues;
- managing the cohort time line of activities;
- supporting and guiding the peer coaches in their work;
- monitoring and moderating the community dialogue;
- nurturing engagement—nudging participants, ensuring questions receive responses;
- collaborating with peer coaches to course correct as needed;
- marketing (internally) and promoting (externally) the community as appropriate;
- training staff and volunteers;

- producing reports on the functioning and metrics of the community; and
- identifying trends within the community and bringing emerging trends from outside the community into community awareness.

Aspects of the role of the online community manager are, of necessity, adaptive because the skills needed to manage a mathematics-only faculty group may be different from those required by a multidisciplinary community. We emphasize the technical proficiency of the community manager because all the work of a pedagogy matters practice improvement community is online and many college faculty are not technically adept. Classroom Notebook is designed to require very little in the way of technological aptitude; however, constant attention behind the scenes is needed to ensure a smooth experience for faculty as issues with browsers, firewalls, and the like always arise. Faculty time is precious, and technical barriers to engagement can harm the community in a multitude of ways.

The community manager is the organizer in chief, skilled in a range of implementation elements, such as communication strategies and engagement activities. The manager makes sure the platform highlights the discussions, resources, guidelines, dates, and policies that are required at any point in time in the community's work. The manager is also the master teacher for the coaches, guiding and supporting them in their circle work and collaborating with them to meet the learning needs of the overall community. The manager must be patient, provide encouragement, and be there to nudge faculty along, all in equal parts.

The community manager watches the community at a metalevel and feeds this perspective back to the community. Some of the things he or she looks for are platform use that has suddenly risen or fallen, a change in the number of compliments or complaints about engagement strategies, and new functionality that might be deployed as the community interaction matures or stabilizes. The community manager has access to the back end of the Classroom Notebook platform, which provides extensive data on the nature of each individual's engagement and metrics on the community overall. This input is invaluable in monitoring the health of the community and in providing qualitative and quantitative data that can be helpful to one community and to the larger field when aggregated.

The community manager focuses on each faculty member in the cohort, looking for the next cadre of coaches, individuals with a particular skill that would benefit the entire community, and, of course, participants who seem to be struggling or falling behind. In sum, the manager is the glue, the wax, and the light, making sure the community remains vibrant by dealing with emergent issues and celebrating what is going well (Crowe, 2013).

Appropriate Technology

We can state unequivocally that for the pedagogy matters practice improvement model, the technology platform is necessary but insufficient to ensure an effective practice improvement experience. Rather, we argue, the design of the routines, the passion of the participants, and the skill of the coaches and community manager, in addition to the technology, are the critical ingredients. Nonetheless, technology does make a difference in how well the work can be done.

While Classroom Notebook has been designed expressly for the pedagogy matters practice improvement model, many platforms and a growing, almost overwhelming, menu of features and options are available and could be adapted to the purpose. When implementing a pedagogy matters practice improvement initiative, the focus should be on technology that deepens reflection, fosters community, and provides ample and robust analytics. As a principle, we believe less is more. We advise focusing on the work at hand and having a small number of excellent customized elements rather than a vast array of bells and whistles.

The pedagogy matters practice improvement model is at its heart dialogic. We give dialogue the broadest interpretation and capitalize on technology to support faculty use of the ever-expanding universe of social tools that serve to diversify and enhance the frequency of sharing, communication, and information discovery. Dialoguing tools in general, and Classroom Notebook in particular, allow for different types of knowledge creation and facilitate community-level reflection. The key for any platform is to enable faculty to cocreate and share knowledge while testing practice.

Negotiables and Nonnegotiables

We have presented a model of practice improvement that is far more than a theoretical construct. It was shaped by faculty, road tested by faculty, and reshaped in response to their experience. However, the design is intentionally malleable for three reasons. First, because each faculty cohort brings its collective context to the work, it is inevitably necessary to adapt aspects of the design to accommodate differences. Second, we really do believe in big data, and we anticipate eagerly the insights that can be derived as a consequence of many faculty members interrogating the design and contributing their experiences to an open data bank. And third, we believe that a dynamic and adaptive community is the only kind of community that will, in fact, elicit deep self-reflective engagement from large numbers of college faculty.

The community manager and the coaches are vital cogs in the feedback loop that can lead to constructive adaptation in response to cohort needs. Collectively, they read everything posted in Classroom Notebook with an eye to the needs of each faculty member, the creative ideas of individuals, and the trends in issues and concerns. Two routines in the design of pedagogy matters are framed specifically to elicit feedback on the practice improvement experience: metareflection and the town hall Jam.

Routine: Metareflection

Metareflection gives faculty an opportunity to synthesize their pedagogy matters experience. This routine, which addresses the same question, adjusted for tense based on when it is posed—What do you hope to get out of this experience? What are you getting out of this experience? What did you get out of this experience?—invites faculty members to share their perspectives with one another and at the same time helps them to integrate their own learning across multiple experiences. Each semester, faculty members write three metareflections; one before the start of the semester, another at midpoint, and the final one at the end. The input from metareflections gives the community manager and coaching team an opportunity to help innovate and further develop the routines of a pedagogy matters community. This openness to change, not only at the level of the individual instructor but also in the work process of the community as a whole, strengthens the sense of a self-guided community. It also allows the professional development processes to advance based on the collective wisdom of the individuals using the tools and routines. Reid Sunahara, an English professor from Hawai'i posted the following midsemester metareflection:

> I really like my pedagogy circle, and I really like this project. I feel like I'm on an all-star team, but I'm sort of the 3rd stringer. I'm a bit younger, and everyone seems so committed and knowledgeable. It's awe inspiring to peek into these courses and the thoughts and work of everyone in this project. . . . I want to talk about what I should be doing, what I'm doing wrong, what I could do better, and of all the feedback I could receive, I value this group more than any other!!! Why wouldn't I?

Routine: Town Hall Jam

As noted in Chapter 4, the pedagogy matters practice improvement model incorporates several cross-disciplinary full-cohort activities, like Jams, to supplement the intense individual classroom practice focus of the model. One specific type of Jam is the town hall, which focuses on pressing issues of concern to the full community about its health and functioning. The format allows faculty to read comments and weigh in as their time permits. As with metareflections, the discussion builds a sense of ownership of and investment in the process and is extremely valuable to the coaches and the community manager. The following is an example of a town hall Jam.

Early in the development of the pedagogy matters practice improvement model, given our desire to see changed and improved practice, we asked the faculty to modify the way they contributed to Peer Practice Dialogue. Instead of a collaborative examination of what was working or not working, we asked each commenting faculty member to suggest how their peers' teaching might improve. We used the following prompt to try to alter the norm:

> Suggest to each of the faculty whose portfolio you reviewed in Week 9 a way that you can see that they might innovate and why. Your suggested innovations should not be strategies that are minimal around the edges improvements, but ones that are at the heart of their teaching, ways that they can strengthen tags or try new ones. Most importantly, when you are making suggestions to others, give specific examples from their portfolios. Look briefly at a few minutes of their videos.

Faculty recoiled at this change. "You've got to be kidding!!!! I don't know how to give this kind of advice," wrote Lori Hirst, an English professor at St. Louis Community College in Missouri. We had violated a profound law in faculty culture. Box L includes posts from a town hall Jam addressing the change in the routine.

Some assert that a critical stance toward how faculty are teaching is necessary for teaching improvement (Yarnall et al., 2010). The pedagogy matters faculty helped us understand that this stance, so common in K–12 teacher training, is based on a presumption of knowledge that is simply not available in higher education. Faculty working with the pedagogy matters practice improvement model want to improve, are clearly engaged, and feel supported by each other in the journey toward pedagogical improvement. However, the leap from closely observing a colleague to suggesting specific changes is too far a distance. Because no pedagogy is perfectly effective and universal, peers have no underlying logic on which to base specific suggestions, even including acknowledging that some strategies are better than others. An "expert" critical stance is in clear violation of the personally expressive dimension of college teaching—professionals who embody expert disciplinary knowledge. If college faculty members receive almost no education in how to teach, they receive even less about how to evaluate others' teaching (which calls into question the thousands of "peer observations" in college classes conducted across the country).

Box L How *Not* to Engage in Peer Practice Dialogue

The last assignment was difficult. It was tough to make suggestions for innovations when I was very impressed with both Kristin's and Yasser's classroom teaching. Plus, the suggestions I gave to them would also be very innovative for my own teaching. I agree with Kathy. I don't know if implementing a certain change, like integrating application models, will affect student success but I feel that it is worth exploring how the connections could be strengthened which might affect student understanding.

La Vache Scanlan, Kapiʻolani Community College, Hawaiʻi

Speaking for myself again, I felt as though I bailed in the last group assignment because I honestly did not know how to recommend the advance of my colleagues' practices.

Christopher Watson, Bunker Hill Community College, Massachusetts

I have thought about it a ton, trying to understand why I have such a hard time with it. I think you are right on when you say it is taboo to tell anyone how to teach. But, while it is taboo, I think there is a reason it is taboo. I have the privilege of teaching with some amazing colleagues. . . . I've watched their classes, created curriculum with them, and even team taught classes with them. Yet, each of us is very different and when I've tried to use some of my colleagues' time-tested techniques in the classroom, they just haven't worked as well when I do them.

Kathy Perrino, Foothill College, California

Although I appreciate your marathon-metaphor, it does not exactly fit. When one is running a marathon and hits the wall, he/she knows what to do: keep running. But we were not only asked to keep running, which we are all doing as fast as we can. Instead, we were asked to look at each other's running and make recommendations for innovations. I know I have never looked at my own work as closely as I do now nor felt the amazing support to do this as I have through this project; nor have I ever had the luxury this project has afforded me to look at the work of others, and reflect on what that means for my own pedagogy; nor have I been able in any other venue to disseminate information about my own changes. I have been able to do that here, and for that I am eternally grateful.

Robin Ozz, Phoenix Community College, Arizona

While painful, our error led to a much-improved design. The town hall Jam discussion resulted in a radical rethinking of how to engage faculty in dialogue about one another's work. We came to understand that there is no one best pedagogical practice for an individual faculty member but rather a set of practices that are artfully applied to the specific needs of the students in front of them, and there is also no obvious better way. Instead, all efforts in a teaching improvement trajectory are wedded to the goals set by each instructor, customized to their personal skills and abilities in the classroom and to the nature of the students sitting before them.

Thus, faculty participants led the pedagogy matters practice improvement community to reject the hypothesis that only critical comments from peers could produce the kinds of pedagogical changes needed to improve student pass rates. Instead, the faculty chose to strengthen the use of tags as the common language for dialogue and analysis of their own and each other's work. The tags ground the collaborative analysis in sufficient detail to provoke deep thinking about what is working and why. The pedagogical pattern then allows an individual instructor to establish goals for improving practice, and the visual pattern gives evidence of progress that can be publicly discussed with peers.

Another consequence of the discussion of peer commenting led us to introduce strategies taken from Cooperrider and Whitney (2005) on appreciative inquiry as a way to solidify the community ethos in commenting.

> I personally look forward to learning more about the Appreciative Inquiry approach as a process to effect change along with any other strategies that will help us achieve our goal. For years I have sought out ways to be a more effective teacher so I am open and appreciative of others' opinions and suggestions. I know that in the end I must decide how to implement suggestions for change in a manner that fits my personality and teaching style. (Katrina Nichols, Delta College, Michigan)

The heart of collective accountability is dialogue. The challenge is to elicit the richest possible exchange and to plumb its depths for the benefit of each individual and the community as a whole.

6

Taking College Teaching Seriously

A Call to Action

I had no opportunity to study higher education in detail before finding myself consumed by its demands. . . . I often look back with some chagrin, realizing how differently I might have acted had I understood then what I only came to appreciate much later.

(Bok, 2013, p. 4)

The centrality of higher education to the future of the world gains momentum with each new report on the state of the social and geopolitical global economy. A digitally driven, knowledge-based, radically connected world demands thinkers, creators, and high-functioning doers. Postsecondary educational attainment is carving a deeper and deeper distinction between people who can participate and thrive in a contemporary context and those who will be marginalized and excluded. The relative balance in any society between those who are participants and those who are on the margin ultimately defines the viability of that society. The stakes for achieving in higher education have never been higher, and it is in this context that we claim in this book that using every possible avenue to increase the

89

number of people who succeed in college demands the elevation of college teaching and its inclusion as a vital part of the solution.

We join the many scholars and practitioners before us, perhaps starting with Ernie Boyer and continuing through the past 40 years, who assert that college teaching is very, very important. We acknowledge the tension between the application and synthesis of knowledge and the creation of new knowledge—the academic divide between teaching and research. Again, like many before us, we want to assert that this divide is not innate to either.

There certainly has been resistance among elements of the higher education community to thinking of pedagogy as a critical skill for college professors. But the reality is that for most college faculty, teaching is a large part of their professional work. Few faculty work only to create new knowledge to the exclusion of teaching undergraduate students. So the questions before us are, What is the best way to define the profession of college teaching? and How do we develop the structures that nurture it? Our response is that the continuous improvement of teaching practices should be thought of as a professional obligation and a personal goal, and research to advance the field of college teaching practice should be judged as critical scholarly research.

What if we *did* take college teaching seriously? What if we aligned processes, support systems, and the affordances of technology to help college faculty improve their practice as we do with medical doctors or architects? What if we acknowledged that good college teaching is not innately or exclusively tied to deep content knowledge but, rather, wedded as well to a fluency in the dynamics of *who* is taught and *how* the teaching is done? What if we had a clear system of practice competency that delineated a path from apprentice to journeyman to master, as we do for intern to resident to attending physician?

To elevate an intentional focus on college teaching we need more than lip service, student satisfaction surveys, scare tactics, or simplistic checklists of actions. Our work finds that faculty members require and respond to customizable approaches embedded in their teaching practice. These approaches must maintain professional autonomy, be supported by a community of peers, and placed within a body of serious research on college teaching.

New Tools for Research on College Teaching

Current technology can now provide the platform on which a new approach to teaching improvement can rest. The capacity to gather data from individual classrooms and to pool those data points across multiple faculty at multiple colleges offers the possibility of creating a quantitative science of college teaching in the same way large data sets have begun to change research and practice in fields such as public health and social science. According to Gary King, director of Harvard's Institute for Quantitative Social Science, "We're really just getting under way. But the march of quantification, made possible by enormous new sources of data, will sweep through academia, business, and government. There is no area that is going to be untouched" (Lohr, 2012, p. SR1).

The serious study of college teaching has been hobbled by the lack of clear metrics, common language, and observational data. With these ingredients in hand, college faculty would be able, as we have demonstrated with the pedagogy practice improvement model, to examine their own teaching and change their behaviors within a trajectory of increasing mastery. However, the bigger payoff to be derived from the digital observation of college teaching will come about when we can look across hundreds or thousands of classrooms and use big data sets to identify patterns. When college faculty log their work, refine the categories of description and analysis, and begin the larger task of systematically linking teaching to learning, a collective scholarly process of practice improvement can result. As with any network or data set, the greater the number of faculty who participate, the greater the ability to capture data, and the more we will see and understand. It is the potential for insights and hypotheses about college teaching provided by emergent patterns of data at scale that holds great promise for improving outcomes for students.

Any research trajectory begins with definitions of the phenomena to be studied and the delineation of research methodology; only some of these prerequisites exist now for research on college teaching. For example, there is no distinctive definition of *college pedagogy*, although Pollard's (2010) definition, with its focus on practice and a shared body of knowledge, or Laurillard's (2002) conversational framework, with its depiction of the inherent complexity of interactions, are good places to start. Laurillard views the development of a serious research trajectory as possible only if those who teach are clearly the agents of change as participants in the process. If clear definitional parameters existed, Laurillard (2008a) suggests that we could create the equivalent of open source technology for college teaching practices. This open source resource would advance college teaching as a field of study, allowing faculty to more carefully design their own work and share one another's, ultimately making innovation in teaching more like the iterative refinement process that characterizes scientific inquiry (Laurillard, 2012). Currently, too few academic faculty who are in a position to evaluate and use the product of the scholarship of pedagogy are engaged in the research, and, therefore, it is unlikely that a body of knowledge will evolve (Devlina & Samarawickremab, 2010; Schulman, 2002). Technology applications, such as the one integrated into the pedagogy matters practice improvement model, are harbingers of a capability that can ignite a true revolution in the art and science of college teaching.

Derek Bok (2013) makes a compelling case for good teaching while acknowledging our current lack of understanding about how to ensure it. However, Bok also reminds us of the skewed funding models that privilege research over teaching (not to mention the skew of support for research institutions over those where teaching dominates) and the folly of that bias.

When Bok (2013) turns his attention to the role of professional schools (specifically medicine, law, and business) he finds a nexus of purpose in *all* professional education that might frame a good beginning for thinking of college teaching as a profession. He suggests that the mission of any professional education is to do the following:

1. Instill the habits of mind characteristic of the profession.
2. Help students acquire specialized information and develop the knowledge needed to apply that knowledge as a practicing professional.
3. Imbue the ethics and responsibility in practice that are central to the profession.

Higher education, like its sister professions of law, medicine, and business, has become more challenging even as student bodies have become increasingly diverse. The knowledge faculty must impart is greater in volume and complexity, and the skills and habits of work they must foster in students as a consequence are more analytically demanding. College teaching under these circumstances is difficult and, it seems clear, requires *both* content and pedagogical proficiency.

We recognize that this is unlikely to be our reality until hiring institutions reward excellent teaching with the same investment they make in their research enterprises. Nonetheless, we can say that in spirit and practice the pedagogy matters practice improvement model embodies Bok's (2013) criteria by offering a specific mental discipline for teaching, specialized knowledge about the process of teaching, and an experience of peer and personal professional responsibility commensurate with the highest levels of professional learning. This is why we see it as an important initial step toward systemic change.

What Technology Can Do: Pedagogy Analytics

We think that a useful and perhaps neglected perspective emerges when we ask what would happen if technology developments were focused on supporting rather than replacing the teacher. While an IBM computer did beat Gary Kasparov, the grand master and World Chess Champion, and the IBM supercomputer Watson did defeat the two top champions of the TV game show *Jeopardy!*, we believe it is more important to appreciate that later contests revealed that technology *plus* people beats technology alone. Technology harnessed to improve college teaching has enormous potential but so little work focuses systematically on helping college faculty teach, the field is grossly underdeveloped. In a Jam on MOOCs (massive open online courses) a participant posted that "there is almost universal agreement that professional development for [teaching] online is important but, interestingly, it is sometimes the first professional development in teaching that faculty have received!"

Technology can give faculty new tools to understand what is happening, and while what we see today is perhaps more vaporware than reality, the promise is significant and investments are being made. The Minerva Project is spending $90 million a year and the educational company Amplify is spending $150 million a year to support teachers in college and high school, demonstrating that venture capitalists are betting that technology will play an increasing role in teaching and that it can return a profit. College faculty ignore at their peril the many fascinating experiments businesses are conducting using technology to deliver instruction. As nonprofit higher education professionals, we don't want the for-profit markets to win and thereby control the focus and delivery of higher education to the world. On the other hand, neither do we want the educational entrepreneurs to lose and thus miss out on the scale, sophistication, and technological firepower brought by private markets. We believe that synergy might profitably evolve if those in higher education embrace a larger system of interaction, one where faculty are centrally involved in the focus and direction of teaching, and market forces gather to scale strategies and develop the technological tools to support them (Lella et al., 2012).

At this time higher education lacks compelling models for leveraging large data sets that yield patterns that can be used to inform innovation in college teaching. However, predictive and learning analytics focused on student behaviors are the first wave of such work (Haythornthwaite, de Laat, & Dawso, 2013; Siemens & Long, 2011), driving analyses of student paths to graduation (Johnson et al., 2013). And faculty hunger for insight and information about the students they teach is widespread. For example, 434 people, primarily faculty and administrators, who posted in a 2013 Jam on predictive analytics, enumerated their view of the top opportunities for applying predictive analytics to their work as follows:

- inform teaching and learning strategies to improve student outcomes;
- predict student outcomes, thereby enabling interventions that promote persistence and completion;

- link individual student's needs to tailored advising and services for personalized interventions;
- examine student behaviors and needs and tie these to patterns of engagement with support services in order to develop "successful" and "at-risk" student profiles; and
- enable early interventions and timely feedback so that interventions are proactive and not reactive (Knowledge in the Public Interest, 2013).

Good work is under way in the learning analytics arena. For example, the Predictive Analytics Reporting Framework was developed to take advantage of emerging decision-making approaches that use business intelligence and data mining techniques to look for student retention patterns across institutions (see www.educause.edu/ero/article/predictive-analytics-reporting-par-framework-wcet). Using more than 1.7 million anonymous student records and 8.1 million institutionally de-identified course-level records, the framework offers educational stakeholders a unique multi-institutional lens for examining dimensions of student success from unified and contextual perspectives. Were we to apply similar methodologies to an examination of teaching, by identifying patterns of behavior across multiple institutions, we could gain insights into teachers and teaching and link these to our emerging understanding of learners and learning.

Why the Instructor Matters

If learning analytics seek to personalize learning and avert attrition, who will help do the personalizing? The data increasingly provide rich material for institutions about their students' specific learning and support needs. In the best circumstances more and more tools are put in the hands of the students themselves to enable them to make key decisions. But at the end of the day, a professor must help each student master content, whatever the discipline, whatever the medium. This is what drives and shapes our work. As a consequence of research and experience with the pedagogy matters practice improvement model, we believe

- pedagogy is critical to the formula of student success;
- faculty want to, can, and should have the opportunity to improve their practice;
- pedagogic data is a by-product of social professional development; and

- pedagogic analytics in the hands of faculty will drive improved teaching and enable practice improvement at scale.

The pedagogy matters practice improvement model is a first iteration of a system that defines and can generate pedagogic data and, thus, makes possible analyses that can inform practice. The design of the model rests on three critical elements to meet this analytic ambition: combining social media with social learning, using patterns derived from data to reveal insights, and structuring learning experiences in an online community. Pedagogic analytics should enable us to see at scale what faculty do and how they do it, where they want or need help, and how their teaching relates to student learning.

The power of great professors is inspirational and aspirational. Faculty move forward the human enterprise of teaching and must be respected and engaged in the process of improvement so that we can energize the entirety of higher education to take college teaching seriously. The following comments from faculty illustrate how an interactive, social, rigorous, and technologically driven professional development experience can support their hard work.

> [The project] is worth far more to me personally and professionally than any single professional development activity in which I have participated in many years. Of course this makes sense because [it] was significantly more substantial than most PD [professional development] in which we engage. (Larry Giddings, Pikes Peak Community College, Colorado)

> I think the continual self-evaluation and reflection allowed us to work together to brainstorm improvements and positive tweaks to be more purposeful in our classrooms as opposed to just randomly reaching in the dark for ideas and techniques in *hope* of success. (Claudia Delgado, Hudson County Community College, New Jersey)

> Speaking as an adjunct, I also have valued the chance to share my teaching and get ideas from others. I can honestly say that this experience has been a life-line of sorts this year. In a "magic wand" instructional setting, I'd wish for the kind of honest, respectful and professionally challenging discussions we have in Classroom Notebook at weekly staff meetings. (Joan Smith, Calhoun Community College, Alabama)

It is our hope that we have made the case in this book that the circumstances of contemporary higher education call for a serious consideration of the role of pedagogy in student learning and the impact of faculty professional improvement on faculty performance.

The Path Forward

For the foreseeable future, technology will not replace the need for excellent teaching, but technology does have a potent role to play in teaching and in faculty professional improvement. Technology makes possible what was never practical or even imaginable. The opportunity before us is to put tools in the hands of faculty to improve teaching. Should we as a nation, through policy and practice, determine to move forward on an agenda that affirms that *pedagogy matters*, we propose three avenues of action: engaging faculty, conducting research, and obtaining data.

Engaging Faculty

The *adjunctification* of college teaching is well documented (see Chapter 1). It is a reality that will not soon change and has important implications for student learning that must be addressed.

> We suggest that much of the student success gap has less to do with the classic stereotype of the harried, distracted, and underpaid part-timer, and far more to do with a lack of institutional intentionality in professional development for part-time faculty, a decided lack of access to institutional resources, and a failure to include these faculty in curricular and policy decisions. (Roney & Ulerick, 2013)

There is a nascent literature on faculty engagement in higher education innovation and change. Two reports are of note: *Engaging Faculty and Staff: An Imperative for Fostering Retention, Advising, and Smart Borrowing* (Texas Guaranteed Student Loan Corporation, 2008) and *Changing the Conversation About Productivity: Strategies for Engaging Faculty and Institutional Leaders* (Kadlec & Friedman, 2012). These reports reinforce the notion that faculty are indispensable parts of initiatives to put changes into practice on college campuses, whether guiding students who must repay their educational loans or leading initiatives that help engage students in the classroom. Our own experience with the pedagogy matters practice improvement model has reinforced our belief that faculty are critical forces in creating the changes needed in college classrooms. Indeed, in our view the project of improving higher education could be enhanced by engaging faculty in at least three ways: involving them in designing and participating in practice improvement, enabling them to provide a pedagogical voice to innovation plans and implementation, and including them in helping to represent the learner experience in conversations about institutional improvement.

Conducting Research

Amundsen and Wilson (2012) conducted an exhaustive review of the literature on what is "variously defined as faculty development, educational development, instructional development, and academic development in higher
education . . . in pursuit of a meaningful basis for investigating the effectiveness of educational development practice" (pp. 90–91). They found that
despite a 30-year literature review, only tentative and weak conclusions about
effectiveness can be drawn, and they called for more rigorous and more qualitative research. They found that the research literature collectively focuses
largely on changing the practices of small groups of faculty, with a few efforts
targeted to the diffusion and uptake of new practices that have been deemed
(but not proven) to be beneficial. Not one study in the literature review
examined the relationship between teaching and student learning.

We believe that focused research on the following questions would contribute significantly to our understanding of how and to what extent pedagogy matters:

1. What is the relationship of teaching to student learning? Within this
   context, lines of inquiry might control for the discipline being taught,
   student demographics, the type of learning modality (e.g., online),
   and other significant elements of the teaching/learning experience. In
   effect, we should determine whether high-quality teaching in higher
   education is a version of the generic brand of good teaching generally, or whether the parameters of good teaching are determined by
   context.
2. Is there a ratio of impact to be discovered? That is, how much does college pedagogy account for student success? As we discussed earlier in
   the book, a mix of curricular, pedagogic, and support elements figure in
   student persistence and success. Is it possible to understand the degree to
   which these elements, separately and in combination, affect the educational outcomes we seek to achieve?
3. What is the impact of professional development on quality teaching as
   defined by improvements in student learning? If, as we state in this book,
   the quality of teaching has an impact on the educational outcomes of students, how can we assess the link between specific professional improvement activities, changes in pedagogy, and student learning?

Figure 6.1 shows the results of the following question on the registration
form for a national Jam held as part of GSCC: In your opinion, what percent of
student success can be attributed to the following (the total must add to 100%)?

1. Pedagogy—Andrew Pollard (2010) defines *pedagogy* as "the practice of teaching framed and informed by a shared and structured body of knowledge" (p. 267).
2. Assessment and Placement—students are assessed accurately and placed into the appropriate developmental education class to acquire the skills they need to be successful in college credit courses.
3. Curriculum—the structure, activities, materials, and sequencing of a course.
4. Support—for personal and academic issues and for college knowledge.
5. Programs—specially designed programs that incorporate some or all of the preceding.

Six hundred and seventy four people, 500 of whom were faculty, answered the question (Yarnall, Feng, Dornsife, Valdes, & Hodge, 2011). We make no assertions about these results because of the nature of the poll. However, the consensus that teaching accounts for roughly 30% of student success seems like a good place to begin the conversation that frames the research on this question. While we don't advocate a deconstructed view of the learning environment, we do think it is important to

Figure 6.1   Jam Participants' Perception of Contributors to Student Success

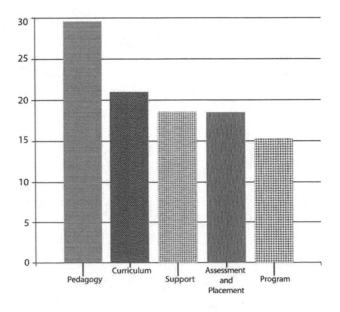

gain a firmer grasp on the impact of teaching in the learning ecosystem. If we can achieve this kind of insight, we might not only rightly value pedagogy, but also gain a keener approach to the allocation of scarce resources.

Obtaining Data

As we have noted, technology is redrawing the landscape of data that is potentially available to us about higher education.

> We are experiencing an unprecedented explosion in the quantity and quality of information available not only to us, but about us. We must adapt individually, institutionally and culturally to the transition in technologies and social norms that makes this possible, and question their impacts. What are the implications of such data availability for learning and knowledge building? (Society for Learning Analytics Research, 2014)

We share the appetite for *learning analytics*, defined in the New Media Consortium's Horizon Report as the "field associated with deciphering trends and patterns from educational big data, or huge sets of student-related data, to further the advancement of a personalized, supportive system of higher education"(Johnson et al., 2013, p. 24). However, we argue that it is imperative that we go beyond where the field is currently focused, which is on ways to personalize learning, prevent student dropouts through early warning systems, and provide students with targeted support. If our preliminary findings about the criticality of pedagogy to student learning are sustained, then there is a world of data that can be created and used by and for faculty to enable them to reflect on their practice in new ways and take increasingly calibrated action to improve their teaching. As Johnson et al (2013) observe,

> learning analytics should not be seen as a short cut to providing teaching professionals with universal advice on "what works." . . . Rather, the most promising area for enhancing teaching practice is the creation of applications which help teachers identify which of the many interventions open to them are most worthy of their attention, as part of an on-going collaborative inquiry into effective practice.

If we had big data on *pedagogical patterns*, as we have defined them in this book, faculty (and others) could mine that data for ongoing iterations of practice improvement.

Final Thoughts

What might a professor's world look like if he or she worked in a place where pedagogy mattered? A world where faculty from across the country (or the globe) used technology to further their own learning, a world where they would hold themselves and their peers to a standard of high rigor for the activities they use in teaching? What might happen if all faculty understood how to pay attention to noncognitive issues in their classrooms? What if each semester they customized their teaching to the specific students in their classes while maintaining fidelity to their own individual personalities and preferences in teaching? How would faculty function if their classrooms were deeply connected to an ongoing social network that helped them frame their actions as issues evolved and were resolved in their classrooms? We, of course, do not know the answer to these questions. But our vision is to continue to nurture a process that supports college faculty in improving their teaching. We hope to connect college faculty nationally and internationally in a social dialogue that enhances their teaching by embedding a practice improvement process into their everyday work. And we believe that such a system is part of the solution to creating higher levels of student success in college.

While many faculty may not be interested in the overall agenda of higher education, a significant enough number of them, when called to action, are eager to step up. For example, in 2011 we held a national Jam as part of GSCC. More than 800 people signed on and explored three topics: instructional strategies, student context, and faculty skills and attributes. The following are comments posted by participants that reflect the high level of interest in these issues:[1]

> The Jam was a good beginning to opening a dialogue on developmental teaching and learning. This exchange is long overdue and should be continued. I would really like to see Interest Groups form as a result of the communication so that we may focus on specialized pedagogy to accomplish different goals in developmental education. Engaging faculty involved in teaching developmental courses nationwide may lead us all to discover viable educational alternatives for developmental students.

> I wanted to thank the organizers of this Jam for their hard work. This was a fantastic experience for me. This is my second year teaching developmental ed classes, and this Jam helped give me perspective on my job. It helped me see some of the struggles I was facing in my teaching were not limited to me or to my classes and that other people had had similar experiences, had dealt with similar questions, and had found creative solutions to the challenges. As an adjunct instructor, it was really nice to be part of a community of people who were as passionate about their students' success

as I was and who had developed creative and inspiring ways to address their students' need. Although I read more of the discussion threads than I actively participated in, I felt like I learned a lot from the other participants, and I feel that I will have more confidence to actively contribute during the next Jam. I am excited to put into practice some of the ideas from the Jam. Thank you for this opportunity!

The concluding discussion of the Jam led to the creation of a pedagogy matters manifesto. We believe that with this manifesto a small group of faculty placed an important stake in the ground for a larger faculty engagement strategy.

Pedagogy Matters! Manifesto

We commit to providing access to outstanding educational opportunities for all students.

We are dedicated to the success of our students, since their success is critical to the prosperity of our communities, our states, our nation, and the global community.

We acknowledge that faculty voices must advocate for innovation and support the achievement of their students. We recognize that in order to meet these goals, we must commit to the pursuit of teaching excellence, demonstrate intentionality, transparency, and effectiveness in our pedagogy, and finally, exhibit passion for the classroom experience.

We pledge to work for the good of the whole student. We acknowledge that developmental education cannot cure the multiple contributors to student failure, including insufficient development prior to college enrollment, poverty, discrimination, and lack of social support. Still, we affirm that informed pedagogy can help students overcome these barriers and achieve deeper learning.

We support our community of engaged professionals to further the cause of improved teaching of developmental education. We believe that to secure a more vibrant role for faculty voice and experience, together we must codify what faculty do, create systems that respect the autonomy of faculty to deliver educational services, and recognize that increasing levels of student success can occur only if faculty are supported in professional development. We further pledge to

- keep student success at the forefront of our practice,
- investigate through evidentiary means the success of our activities in the classroom and share the results of this assessment,

- reflect upon our own teaching practices in conversation with other developmental education professionals, and
- pledge to advance pedagogy as an important part of graduate education for future faculty.

We must be fully invested in initiatives seeking to improve student learning, and to that end we pledge to

- educate ourselves in effective ways to represent our practice to stakeholders: students, families, voters, politicians, and media; and
- participate actively in the democratic processes to represent our work.

We, therefore, representing ourselves as engaged professionals, do solemnly publish and declare that a developmental education pedagogy, which incorporates the ideals and ideas cited previously, be a part of our ongoing national conversation.

Note

1. All quotes are taken from the 2011 Jam and names withheld for privacy.

APPENDIX

Tags: Origins and Definitions

The tags were created after the first semester of the project with Cohort 1 faculty who were selected for participation through nomination by the college presidents from a group of leading community colleges chosen because of their reputation. Additionally, the 25 faculty (13 English faculty members and 12 mathematics faculty members, one of whom withdrew in the middle of the first semester because of illness) were certified as having developmental course pass rates in the top 10% of all faculty at their college.

Tags were generated from the first semester's compendium of richly detailed descriptive and analytic work. The classroom practice of the highly effective faculty was captured digitally and was therefore available for analysis. There was a fire hose of digital data from the first semester. If each page of the online postings were printed, including the classroom narrative practice and reflection (with attendant postings of classroom activities and student work), group activities, dialogue in smaller pedagogy circles, and the open-space coffee klatch, the document would run into more than 1,200 pages. These data were submitted for a qualitative analysis of themes (Pope, Ziebland, & Mays, 2000). A standard qualitative analysis of the textual data was deductively performed using a grounded-theory approach. The first level of analysis was conducted by one member of the project team who was trained in qualitative analysis and who produced the first categories. She reviewed more than 50 individual faculty teaching portfolio postings and identified 19 categories of developmental education pedagogy. The second level of initial categorization was conducted by four additional members of the project team, each reviewing the portfolios of six faculty from a single pedagogy circle. This sequential analysis slightly refined the 19 categories and added seven categories, producing a total of 26 categories which would ultimately be used as tags. (The tags were refined further over time.) The third level of analytic induction was conducted by external evaluators from SRI International, who cross-mapped

103

the instructional approaches represented by the tags with a literature review of developmental education and organized the 31 discrete tags into a set of five themes (Yarnall, Feng, Dornsife, Werner, et al., 2011).

The final stage of creating an authoritative list entailed vetting the tags further in two ways. First, project faculty reviewed the categories, affirming that the categories appeared to be comprehensive and accurate. Second, student voices were incorporated into the project through a moderated asynchronous online student Jam (Kaulback, 2010). One hundred and eighty-three students from the classes of project faculty participated in the Jam. Their responses to the question, "What does your instructor do that makes him/her an effective teacher?" were analyzed. The external evaluators determined that students' responses also aligned with the categorical analysis of project faculty pedagogy (Yarnall, Feng, Fusco, et al., 2011). Tagging is a process used frequently by online writers as a way to create keywords for aggregation of content across multiple postings. In the project, the tags evolved into an authoritative set of knowledge tags, forming a higher order classification system.

The project faculty then instituted tagging in the second semester of their work, so the tag analysis began at that point. "Faculty tagged a lesson, usually by noting in parentheses in their Digication e-Portfolios the precise point in the lesson that represented the pedagogical theme tag" (Yarnall, Feng, Fusco, et al., 2011, p. 38). SRI International evaluated the compliance with the tagging routine, noting that faculty tended to tag about five times per week.

The accuracy of self-tagging was evaluated by SRI International, which examined the validity in two phases. First, expert evaluators compared their tags with faculty tags in the weekly classroom narratives, with interrater reliability at 83%. A lower level of interrater reliability was found for the tagging of videos, 75% for the majority of videos reproduced. The evaluators attributed the lower level to several factors, including the inability of expert raters to agree on the appropriate tag or a tag representing introspective or affective dimensions (such as caring), which are difficult to ascertain visually.

SRI International evaluators found a correlation between tagging and intermediate positive outcomes such as adapting or adopting practices from peers ($r = .515$, $n = 25$, $P = .008$), or innovating new ones ($r = .587$, $n = 25$, $P = .003$). Tagging was also correlated with using formative classroom assessment techniques (CATs) across all semesters ($r = .640$, $n = 25$, $P = .002$). High correlation between total tags and pass rates was also found ($r = .561$, $n = 25$, $P < .01$). An SRI International faculty survey also found that faculty overwhelmingly agreed with the statement that the tags provided a useful vocabulary for describing pedagogy.

Tag data were also evaluated on whether they were distinctive by discipline (math or English). English faculty used a greater total number of tags than math faculty did—it should be noted that English faculty tend to write more detailed text. We were also able to observe a slight tendency for some tags to be grouped together, for example, a biplot shows that math faculty tend to be on the positive side of the high-structure axis while English faculty tend to be on the positive side of the high-cognition axis. Tag distribution was not significantly associated with discipline.

Final Set of Tags by Themes Currently in Use

The set of tags, organized into five major themes, can be found at https://takingcollegeteachingseriously.kpublic.net/home. The set of tags has slightly evolved over the entire five-year project as more data are generated and analysis of faculty teaching behaviors occurs. (The original set of 31 tags can be found in Yarnall, Feng, Dornsife, Werner, et al., 2011.) The following listing shows the 20 tags faculty use to identify their teaching behaviors. All tags under a single theme represent different actions that faculty use in a classroom that express the overall theme in action. Each tag is defined.

Theme I: Creating a Supportive *Classroom Environment*

Tags: Definitions

Caring. Instructors show students that they care about their success in the class by seeking to create a personal connection with individual students. This could manifest itself through personal conversations, offering advice, e-mail contacts, and sharing stories from the teachers' own personal experience. Instructors get to know their students, taking into consideration students' real-life experiences, self-concepts, cultural differences, learning challenges, and the nonacademic difficulties that can affect students' academic performance. Instructors take action to stay in touch with students inside and outside class.

Community Building. Instructors create activities that require students to interact with one other to encourage community building, collaboration, and engagement. Activities are low stakes and not graded.

Transition to College. Instructors help students develop a sense of self-efficacy about being a college student, thereby supporting their transition to college. Examples include encouraging regular attendance, completion of assigned work, and participation in class activities as well as lessons on study skills and familiarization with college services (such as advisement and counseling). Instructors lead the students to an understanding of choice and the inevitable consequences of choices.

Inclusiveness. Instructors create an inclusive environment by designing activities to meet the varying needs of all students, track students and their progress, and reach out to students who are struggling or unable to keep up. Instructors encourage students to participate in class by making the classroom a safe and comfortable space for students to ask questions or make mistakes.

Enjoyment. Instructors create enjoyable classroom activities such as games, debates, field trips, and such to create a fun environment that is conducive to learning.

Theme II: Creating a Varied Classroom Environment

Tags: Definitions

Differentiated Instruction. Instructors use a mix of activities within the same class session, such as lecture, discussion, small-group work, student pairs, use of technology, and so on, with the goal of designing activities to meet the diverse needs of all students.

Multimodal Instruction. Instructors present the same information using a variety of modes, such as visual, oral, aural, experiential, hands on, and so forth. This may include multiple ways of problem solving for one problem.

Contextualization. Instructors make sense of theoretical material by applying it to situations either in the real world or in another academic context. Examples of this might be amortizing a mortgage, selecting the best cell phone plan, writing letters of application, and writing research papers.

Collaboration. Instructors create community by designing collaborative projects that require students to work together in order to learn. This can be done during a segment of class, over the course of an entire class period, or outside class.

Adaptability. Instructors reflect on their teaching practices and student needs, changing their methods, timing, and activities, as needed. This might happen from class to class, or even within a class, when the instructor perceives that the current strategy is not working.

Theme III: Creating a Challenging Classroom Environment

Tags: Definitions

Higher Order Thinking. Instructors use specific approaches to engage students in critical thinking, complex problem solving, analytical reasoning, abstract reasoning, and deductive or inductive thinking. Instructors have students defend and justify positions.

Self-Reflection. Instructors create opportunities for students to assess their own work, allowing them to identify their strengths and weaknesses and make adjustments to their learning strategies. This often involves meta-cognition where students are asked to make an analysis of the discipline they are trying to master and how this mastery may be obtained.

High Expectations. Instructors set high standards for the learning objectives, taking into consideration the current skill level of the students. Instructors develop ways to push students beyond their self-perceived limits.

Theme IV: Creating an Organized *Classroom Environment*

Tags: Definitions
Structured Lessons. Instructors present ideas in a logical progression and provide guidance on how to complete assignments, perhaps modeling them or providing a rubric. Instructors break down complex ideas to make them understandable to all students.

Connections. Instructors help students make connections between the topics/ideas within the course and their prior knowledge/experience. This may involve the instructor showing how concepts within the content area are related and helping students link related concepts in a discipline and between earlier and later work in a class.

Time on Task. Instructors create challenging learning activities that maximize practice and student attention to task, providing class time for students to practice the desired skills.

Scaffolding. Instructors scaffold assignments by providing a sequential set of activities (including low, medium, and high stakes) that build on one another and help move students toward increasing levels of sophistication in their work. Scaffolding is removed as students show evidence of independent performance. This is about finding the optimal challenge for students as they progress.

Theme V: Evaluating *Student Work*

Tags: Definitions
Baseline Knowledge. Instructors evaluate what students know at the beginning of the course, course segment, or day's lesson to create a baseline of student knowledge that can later be compared to what students know at the end of the course, course segment, or day's lesson.

Assessment. Instructors use assessment tools to gauge student progress and share the results of those assessments with students to help them understand how well they are mastering the material.

Feedback. Instructors review student work and provide timely, constructive, ungraded feedback in conversation or writing. It resembles coaching and is known as formative feedback.

REFERENCES

Amundsen, C., & Wilson, M. (2012). Are we asking the right questions? A conceptual review of the educational development literature in higher education. *Review of Educational Research, 82*(90), 90–126.

Angelo, T. A., & Cross, K. P. (1993). *Classroom assessment techniques: A handbook for college teachers* (2nd ed.). San Francisco, CA: Jossey-Bass.

Arcario, P., Bret, E., Klages, M., & Polnariev, B. A. (2013). Closing the loop: How we better serve our students through a comprehensive assessment process. *Metropolitan Universities Journal, 24*(2), 21–37.

Association of American Colleges & Universities. (2007). *College learning for the new global century: Liberal education and America's promise.* Washington, DC: Author.

Athey, R. (2001). *Collaborative knowledge networks: Driving workforce performance through Web-enabled communities.* Retrieved from http://www.ickn.org/documents/eview.pdf

Barker, I. (2005). *What is information architecture?* Retrieved from http://www.steptwo.com.au/papers/kmc_whatisinfoarch/

Bass, R. (2012a). Disrupting ourselves: The problem of learning in higher education. *EDUCAUSE Review, 47*(2), 23–33.

Bass, R. (2012b, March). *The 21st century learner: A holistic approach.* Paper presented at the opening sessions of the meeting at LaGuardia Community College, Long Island City, NY.

Bierman, S., Ciner, E., Lauer-Glebov, J., Rutz, C., & Savina, M. (2005). Integrative learning: Coherence out of chaos. *Peer Review, 7*(4), 18–20.

Bok, D. (2006). *Our underachieving colleges: A candid look at how much students learn and why they should be learning more.* Princeton, NJ: Princeton University Press.

Bok, D. (2013). *Higher education in America.* Princeton, NJ: Princeton University Press.

Booth, S. (2011). *Cultivating knowledge sharing and trust in online communities for educators: A multiple case study.* Retrieved from http://connectededucators.org/wp-content/uploads/2011/03/0143_OCoP-Design-Guidelines-March-2011.pdf

Bowen, W. G., Chingos, M. M., & McPherson, M. S. (2009). *Crossing the finish line: Completing college at America's public universities.* Princeton, NJ: Princeton University Press.

Boyer, E. (1990). *Scholarship reconsidered: Priorities of the professoriate.* Princeton, NJ: Princeton University Press and The Carnegie Foundation for the Advancement of Teaching.

Brookfield, S. D. (1995). *Becoming a critically reflective teacher.* San Francisco, CA: Jossey-Bass.

Brownell, J., & Swaner, L. E. (2009). High-impact practices: Applying the learning outcomes literature to the development of successful campus programs. *Peer Review, 11*(2), 26–30.

Cambridge, D., Kaplan, S., & Suter, V. (2005). *Step-by-step guide for designing and cultivating communities of practice.* Retrieved from http://net.educause.edu/ir/library/pdf/nli0531.pdf

Carnevale, A. P., & Strohl, J. (2010). How increasing college access is increasing inequality, and what to do about it. In R. D. Kahlenberg (Ed.), *Rewarding strivers: Helping low-income students succeed in college* (pp. 71–190). New York, NY: Century Foundation Press.

Century Foundation Task Force on Preventing Community Colleges From Becoming Separate and Unequal. (2013). *Bridging the higher education divide: Strengthening community colleges and restoring the American dream.* New York, NY: Century Foundation Press.

Chickering, A., & Reisser, L. (1993). *Education and identity.* San Francisco, CA: Jossey-Bass.

Chickering, A., & Gamson, Z. (1987). Seven principles of good practice in undergraduate education. *AAHE Bulletin, 39,* 3–7.

Chickering, A. W., & Gamson, Z. F. (1991). Seven principles for good practice in undergraduate education. *New Directions for Teaching and Learning, 1991*(47), 63–69.

Cioffi-Revilla, C. (2010). Computational social science. *Computational Statistics, 2*(3), 259–271.

Clouder, L., Broughan, C., Jewell, J., & Steventon, G. (Eds.). (2012). *Improving student engagement and development through assessment: Theory and practice in higher education.* Florence, KY: Routledge, Taylor & Francis.

Clyburn, G. M. (2013). Improving on the American Dream: Mathematics pathways to student success. *Change, 45*(5), 15–23.

Cook, B. (2011, November). *Reforming IPEDs: Creating more accuracy about national college students.* Paper presented at the meeting of the National Attainment Committee, Washington, DC.

Cooperrider, D. L., & Whitney, D. (2005). *Appreciative inquiry: A positive revolution in change.* San Francisco, CA: Berrett-Koehler.

Crowe, R. (2013). *Two key questions for every community manager.* Retrieved from http://www.socialfish.org/search/community+manager

D'Antonio, A., Barnhardt, J., & Greto, V. (2013, March). *Psychological perspectives from a media-use study: Are cell phones and technology changing college students?* Paper presented at the meeting of NASPA–Student Affairs Professionals in Higher Education, Orlando, FL.

D'Avanzo, C. (2009). Supporting faculty through a new teaching and learning center. *AAC&U Peer Review, 11*(2), 22–25.

Devlina, M., & Samarawickremab, G. (2010). The criteria of effective teaching in a changing higher education contex. *Higher Education Research & Development, 29*(2), 111–124.

Dewey, J. (1910). *How we think.* New York, NY: D. C. Heath.

Ellison, N., Weber, M., & Gibbs, J. (2013, April). *The role of social media for knowledge sharing and collaboration in distributed teams.* Paper presented at the meeting of the Collaborative Organizations and Social Media, Brunswick, ME. Retrieved from http://digitalcommons.bowdoin.edu/cgi/viewcontent.cgi?article=1021&context=cosm

Farooq, U., Schank, P., Harris, A., Fusco, J., Schlager, M. S., Harris, P., . . . Schlager, M. (2009). Sustaining a community computing infrastructure for online teacher professional development: A case study of designing tapped in. In J. M. Caroll (Ed.), *Interdisciplinary perspectives on human centered information technology* (pp. 111–138). Menlo Park, CA: Springer.

Fayer L., Zalud, G., Baron, M., Anderson, C. M., & Duggan, T. J. (2011). Student perceptions of the use of inquiry practices in a biology survey laboratory course. *Journal of College Science Teaching, 41*(2), 82–88.

Fini, A. (2008). E-Learning 2.0. A case study on a growing community. *Journal of e-Learning and Knowledge Society, 4*(3), 167–175.

Fluckiger, J., Tixier y Vigil, Y., Pasco, R. J., & Danielson, K. E. (2010). Formative feedback: Involving students as partners in assessment to enhance learning. *College Teaching, 58*(4), 136–140.

Fong, B. C. (2014). *Steering committee meeting February 4–5.* Palo Alto, CA: Carnegie Foundation for Teaching and Learning.

Fontaine, M. A. (2002). *Overcoming knowledge barriers with communities of practice.* Armonk, NY: IBM Corporation.

Foroughi, A. (2011). A research framework for evaluating the effectiveness of implementations of social media in higher education. *Online Journal of Workforce Education and Development, 5*(1), 1–12.

Garner, R. (2006). Humor in pedagogy: How ha-ha can lead to aha! *College Teaching, 54*(1), 177–180.

Giroux, H. (1991). *Postmodernism, feminism, and cultural politics: Redrawing educational boundaries.* Albany, NY: SUNY Press.

Grubb, W. N. E. (1999). *Honored but invisible.* New York, NY: Routledge.

Gruzd, A., Haythornthwaite, C., Paulin, C. A., Absar, R., & Huggett, M. (2014, March). *Learning analytics for the social media age.* Paper presented at the Fourth International Conference on Learning Analytics & Knowledge, Indianapolis, IN.

Halpern, D. F. (1994). Rethinking college instruction for a changing world. In D. F. Halpern (Ed.), *Changing college classrooms: New teaching and learning strategies for an increasingly complex world* (pp. 1–10). San Francisco, CA: Jossey-Bass.

Haswell, R. H. (2008). Teaching of writing in higher education. In C. Bazerman (Ed.), *Handbook of research on writing: History, society, school, individual, text* (pp. 405–424). New York, NY: Erlbaum.

Hattie, J., & Marsh, H. W. (1996). The relationship between research and teaching: A meta-analysis. *Review of Educational Research, 66*(4), 507–542.

Haythornthwaite, C., de Laat, M., & Dawso, S. (2013). Introduction to the special issue on learning analytics. *American Behavioral Scientist, 57*(10), 1371–1379.

Hildreth, P. M., & Kimble, C. (Eds.). (2004). *Knowledge networks: Innovation through communities of practice.* London, UK: Idea Group.

Huber, M. T., & Hutchings, P. T. (2005). *The advancement of learning: Building the teaching commons.* San Francisco, CA: Jossey-Bass.

Hutchings, P. (1993). *Using cases to improve college teaching: A guide to more reflective practice.* Washington, DC: American Association for Higher Education.

Hutchings, P. (1998). The course portfolio: How faculty can examine their teaching to advance practice and improve student learning. In P. Hutchings (Ed.), *The teaching initiatives* (pp. 88–103). Washington, DC: American Association for Higher Education.

Hutchings, P., & Schulman, L. (1999). The scholarship of teaching: New elaborations, new developments. *Change, 31*(5), 10–15.

Johnson, L., Adams Becker, S., Cummins, M., Estrada, V., Freeman, A., & Ludgate, H. (2013). *NMC horizon report: 2013 higher education edition.* Austin, TX: The New Media Consortium.

Johnson Foundation. (1989a). *Principles for good practice in undergraduate education: Faculty inventory.* Racine, WI: Author.

Johnson Foundation. (1989b). *Principles for good practice in undergraduate education: Institutional inventory.* Racine, WI: Author.

Kadlec, A., & Friedman, W. (2012). *Changing the conversation about productivity: Strategies for engaging faculty and institutional leaders.* New York, NY: Public Agenda.

Kagan, D. D. (1992). Implication of research on teacher belief. *Educational Psychologist, 27*(1), 65–90.

Kanpol, B. (1992). The politics of similiarity within difference: A pedagogy of the other. *The Urban Review, 24*(2), 105–131.

Karp, M. M., Hughes, K. L., & O'Gara, L. (2010). An exploration of Tinto's integration framework for community college students. *Journal of College Student Retention: Research, Theory and Practice, 12*(1), 69–88.

Katzenbach, J. R., Steffen, I., & Kronley, C. (2012). Cultural change that sticks. *Harvard Business Review, 90*(7), 110–117.

Kaulback, B. (2010). *Global Skills for College Completion (GSCC) student Jam on community college teaching and learning.* Brooklyn, NY: Knolwedge in the Public Interest.

Keitt, T. (2011). *Psion embraces intercompany collaboration as a core part of its business.* Cambridge, MA: Forrester.

Kember, D., & Leung, D. (2009). Development of a questionnaire for assessing students' perceptions of the teaching and learning environment and its use in quality assurance. *Learning Environments Research, 12*(1), 15–29.

Knowledge in the Public Interest. (2013). *Momentum brief on predictive analytics.* New York, NY: Author.

Kuh, G. D. (2007). What student engagement data tell us about college readiness. *Peer Review, 9*(1), 4–8.

Kuh, G. D. (2008). *High-impact educational practices: What they are, who has access to them, and why they matter.* Washington, DC: American Association of Colleges & Universities.

Kuh, G. D. (2009). What student affairs professionals need to know about student engagement. *Journal of College Student Development, 50*(6), 683–706.

Laksova, K., Mann, S., & Dahlgrena, L. O. (2008). Developing a community of practice around teaching: A case study. *Higher Education Research & Development, 27*(2), 121–132.

Laurillard, D. (2002). *Rethinking university teaching: A conversational framework for the effective use of learning technologies* (2nd ed.). London, UK: RoutledgeFalmer.

Laurillard, D. (2008a). Open teaching: The key to sustainable and effective open education. In T. K. Iiyoshi & M. S. Vijay (Ed.), *Open content, and open knowledge* (pp. 319–335). Cambridge; MA: MIT Press.

Laurillard, D. (2008b). The teacher as action researcher: Using technology to capture pedagogic form. *Studies in Higher Education, 33*(2), 139–154.

Laurillard, D. (2012). *Teaching as a design science: Building pedagogical patterns for learning and technology.* New York, NY: Routledge.

Laurillard, D., & Masterman, L. (2010, July). *Implementing a constructionist approach to collaboration through a learning design support environment.* Paper presented at the European LAMS Conference, Oxford, UK.

Lave, J., & Wenger, E. (1991). *Situated learning: Legitimate peripheral participation.* Cambridge, UK: Cambridge University Press.

Lazer, D., Pentland, A., Adamic, L., Aral, S., Barabási, A.-L., Brewer, D., . . . Van Alstyne, M. (2009). Computational social science. *Science, 323*(5915), 721–723.

Lella, G., Fischetto, A., Cesarotti, V., Spohrer, J. C., Ren, G., & Leung, Y. (2012, July). *Universities as complex service systems: External and internal perspectives.* Paper presented at the 2012 IEEE International Conference on Service Operations and Logistics and Informatics, Suzhou, China.

Lieberman, D. (2005). Beyond faculty development: How centers for teaching and learning can be laboratories for learning. *New Directions for Higher Education, 2005*(131), 87–98.

Lohr, S. (2012, February 11). The age of big data. *The New York Times,* p. SR1.

Luke, A., & Luke, C. (1990). Knowledge as simulation: Curriculum in postmodern conditions. *Discourse: Studies in the Cultural Politics of Education, 10*(2), 91–105.

Lyons, N. (2010). *Handbook of reflection and reflective inquiry: Mapping a way of knowing for professional reflective inquiry.* London, UK: Springer.

Matlin, M. W. (2002). Cognitive psychology and college-level pedagogy: Two siblings that rarely communicate. *New Directions for Teaching and Learning, 2002*(89), 87–103.

McKlenney, K. (2006). *Community college survey of student engagement.* Retrieved from http://www.ccsse.org/

Mellow, G. (2013). *Review of the journal* College Teaching *(1985–2005) and* New Directions for Teaching and Learning *(1985–2010).* New York, NY: LaGuardia Community College.

Mellow, G. O., Woolis, D. D., & Laurillard, D. (2011). In search of a new developmental education pedagogy. *Change, 43*(3), 50–59.

Mentkowski, M., Rogers, G., Doherty, A., Loacker, G., Hart, J. R., Rickards, W., . . . Roth, J. (2000). *Learning that lasts: Integrating learning, development, and performance in college and beyond.* San Francisco, CA: Jossey-Bass.

Mezirow, J. (1990). How critical reflection triggers transformative learning. In J. Mezirow (Ed.), *Fostering critical reflection in adulthood* (pp. 1–20). San Francisco, CA: Jossey-Bass.

Mullins, C. (2013). 2012 distance education survey results. In F. Lokken and C. Mullins (Ed.), *Trends in eLearning: Tracking the impact of elearning at community colleges* (pp. 12–34). Washington DC: Instructional Technology Council.

National Center for Education Statistics. (2013). *Characteristics of postsecondary students spring 2012, enrollment component.* Retrieved from http://nces.ed.gov/programs/coe/indicator_csb.asp

National Governors Association Center for Best Practices & the Council of Chief State School Officers. (2010). *Common core state standards.* Washington, DC: Author.

National Survey of Student Engagement. (2013). About NSSE. Retrieved from http://nsse.iub.edu/html/about.cfm

New Media Consortium. (2013). *NMC horizon report: 2013 higher education edition.* Austin, TX: New Media Consortium and EDUCAUSE.

Owyang, J. (2008). *Forrester reports: Online community best practices.* Retrieved from http://www.web-strategist.com/blog/2008/02/14/forrester-report-online-community-best-practices/

Pascarella, E., & Terenzeni, P. (2005). *How college affects students: A third decade of research* (2nd ed.). San Franciso, CA: Jossey-Bass.

Perin, D. (2000). *Curriculum and pedagogy to integrate occupational and academic instruction in the community college: Implications for faculty development.* New York, NY: Teachers College.

Pollard, A. (2010). *Professionalism and pedagogy: A contemporary opportunity.* London, UK: University of London.

Pope, C., Ziebland, S., & Mays, N. (2000). Analysing qualitative data. *BMJ, 320*(7277), 114–116.

Porchea, S. F., Allen, J. R., & Phelps, R. P. (2010). Predictors of long-term enrollment and degree outcomes for community college students: Integrating academic, psychosocial, socio-demographic, and situational factors. *The Journal of Higher Education, 81*(6), 750–778.

Ratcliff, J. L., Jones, E. A., Guthrie, D. S., & Oehler, D. (1991). *The effect of coursework patterns, advisement, and course selection on the development of general learned abilities of college graduates: Final report.* University Park, PA: Pennsylvania State University.

Riehlea, C., & Weinera, S. (2013). High-impact educational practices: An exploration of the role of information literacy. *College & Undergraduate Libraries, 20*(2), 127–143.

Rodgers, C. (2002). Defining reflection: Another look at John Dewey and reflective thinking. *Teachers College Record, 104*(4), 842–866.

Roney, K., & Ulerick, S. L. (2013). A roadmap to engaging part-time faculty in high-impact practices. *Peer Review, 15*(3). Retrieved from https://aacu.org/peerreview/2013/summer/roney-ulerick

Rosenbush, S. (2013). Data visualization helps Safeway improve inventory management. Retrieved from *Wall Street Journal* website: http://deloitte.wsj.com/cio/2013/12/03/data-visualization-helps-safeway-improve-inventory-management/

Rouseff-Baker, F. (2002). Leading change through faculty development. *New Directions for Community Colleges, 2002*(12), 35–42.

Schön, D. A. (1978). *Educating the reflective practitioner: Toward a new design for teaching and learning in the professions.* San Francisco, CA: Jossey-Bass.

Schön, D. A. (1983). *The reflective practitioner: How professionals think in action.* New York, NY: Basic Books.

Schulman, L. (2002). From Minsk to Pinsk: Why a scholarship of teaching and learning? *The Journal of Scholarship of Teaching and Learning, 1*(1), 48–52.

Senge, P. (2006). *The fifth discipline: The art and practice of the learning organization.* New York, NY: Doubleday.

Shaffer, F. P. (2011). *A guide to academic freedom.* Washington, DC: Association of Governing Boards.

Siemens, G., & Long, P. (2011). Penetrating the fog: Analytics in learning and education. *EDUCAUSE Review, 46*(5), 30–32.

Society for Learning Analytics Research. (2014). *Mission statement.* Retrieved from http://solaresearch.org/about/

Summers, J. J., Beretvas, S. N., Svinicki, M. D., & Gorin, J. S. (2005). Evaluating collaborative learning and community. *The Journal of Experimental Education, 73*(3), 165–188.

Sun, H., & Chen, L. (2014). A framework for analysing the social affordance of Web 2.0 tools. *International Journal of Social Media and Interactive Learning Environments, 2*(1), 37–59.

Survey, C. P. (2011). *Characteristics of postsecondary students.* Washington, DC: U.S. Census Bureau.

Tagg, J. (2012). Why does the faculty resist change? *Change, 44*(4), 6–15.

Tess, P. A. (2013). The role of social media in higher education classes (real and virtual): A literature review. *Computers in Human Behavior, 29*(5), A60–A68.

Texas Guaranteed Student Loan Corporation. (2008). *Engaging faculty and staff: An imperative for fostering retention, advising, and smart borrowing.* Round Rock, TX: Author.

Tompkins, J. (1990). Pedagogy of the distressed. *College English, 52*(6), 653–660.

Trowler, V. (2010). *Student engagement literature review*. York, UK: Higher Education Academy, Lancaster University.

Twombly, S. T., & Townsend, B. K. (2008). Community college faculty: What we know and need to know. *Community College Review, 36*(1), 5–24.

Wagner, D., Vollmar, G., & Wagner, H.-T. (2014). The impact of information technology on knowledge creation: An affordance approach to social media. *Journal of Enterprise Information Management, 27*(1), 31–44.

Wenger, E. (1998). *Communities of practice: Learning, meaning, and identity*. Cambridge, UK: Cambridge University Press.

Wenger-Trayner, B., & Wenger-Trayner, E. (2014). *Introduction to communities of practice*. http://wenger-trayner.com/?s=communities+of+practice&x=0&y=0

Woolis, D., & Restler, S. (2014). *What's an eCommunity?* Retrieved from http://www.kpublic.com/ecommunity/

Yarnall, L., Feng, M., Dornsife, C., Valdes, K., & Hodge, L. (2011). *Jam report. Pedagogy matters: Perspectives of community college developmental educators*. Palo Alto, CA: SRI International.

Yarnall, L., Feng, M., Dornsife, C., Werner, A., Fusco, J., Tidwell-Morgan, E., . . . Gallagher, L. (2011). *Seeing pedagogy: Affordances of an online professional development system for individual faculty improvement*. Palo Alto, CA: SRI International.

Yarnall, L., Feng, M., Fusco, J., Tidwell-Morgan, E., Ngo, F., Werner, A., . . . Dornsife, C. (2011). *Classroom practice in the cloud: Designing an online network for developmental educators*. Palo Alto, CA: SRI International.

Yarnall, L., Gallagher, L., Fusco, J., Remold, J., Schank, P., Feng, M., . . . Tidwell-Morgan, E. (2010). *Pedagogical patterns in the global skills for college completion project: Second semester formative evaluation*. Palo Alto, CA: SRI International.

York, P. (2011). *Success by design*. New York, NY: TCC Group.

INDEX

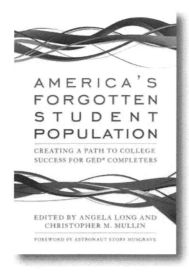

America's Forgotten Student Population

Creating a Path to College Success for GED® Completers

Edited by Angela Long and Christopher M. Mullin

Foreword by Story Musgrave

"This important book provides a rich set of perspectives on the needs, aspirations, and, yes, potential for success of an often neglected population of college students: those who earned a GED instead of a high school diploma. It is a must-read for college educators who want to understand who these students are and how better to serve them."

—*Davis Jenkins*, *Senior Research Associate, Community College Research Center, Teachers College, Columbia University*

This book is a comprehensive resource for college administrators, educational policy makers, and researchers, offering both broad policy recommendations and tested ideas and models that can be implemented at the state and institutional level.

22883 Quicksilver Drive
Sterling, VA 20166-2102

Subscribe to our e-mail alerts: www.Styluspub.com

Taking College Teaching Seriously

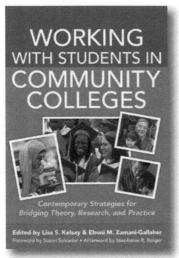

Working With Students in Community Colleges

Contemporary Strategies for Bridging Theory, Research, and Practice

Edited by Lisa S. Kelsay and Eboni M. Zamani-Gallaher

Foreword by Susan Salvador

Afterword by Stephanie R. Bulger

"Once in a while, a book forces us to reconsider the fundamentals of our practices and that book is *Working With Students in Community Colleges*. This volume fills a void in the current literature and is a must-read for anyone struggling to understand the current dilemmas in community colleges. It will inform and prepare graduate students in higher education administration, counseling, and student affairs programs. Faculty and graduate students can build on research questions introduced in this volume. This volume is an indispensable tool in the administrator's toolkit and will be well used as we go boldly into the future."

—*Stephanie R. Bulger, District Vice Chancellor of Educational Affairs, Wayne County Community College District*

(Continues on preceding page)